COPING
WITH
PARENTS

PETER COREY

Illustrated by Martin Brown

Hippo Books
Scholastic Children's Books
London

For
Arthur and Grace
without whom
this book would
have to have been
written by
someone
else

Scholastic Children's Books
Scholastic Publications Ltd,
7–9 Pratt Street, London NW1 0AE, UK

Scholastic Inc.,
730 Broadway, New York, NY 10003, USA

Scholastic Canada Ltd,
123 Newkirk Road, Richmond Hill,
Ontario, Canada L4C 3G5

Ashton Scholastic Pty. Ltd,
P O Box 579, Gosford, New South Wales,
Australia

Ashton Scholastic Ltd,
Private Bag 1, Penrose, Auckland,
New Zealand

First published by
Scholastic Publications Ltd, 1989

Text copyright © Peter Corey, 1989
Illustrations copyright © Martin Brown 1989

ISBN 0 590 76140 4

All rights reserved

Made and printed by Cox & Wyman Ltd.,
Reading, Berks.

Typeset in Plantin by COLLAGE (Design in Print)
Longfield Hiil, Kent

10 9 8 7 6 5 4 3

CONTENTS

Do You Need This Book?

IN ORDER TO WORK OUT WHETHER OR NOT YOU NEED THIS BOOK, DO THIS SIMPLE QUIZ:

1. A parent is:
   A) a mother or father
   B) a type of cheese
   c) a loud noise

2. A parent is usually:
   A) older than you
   B) younger than you
   C) made of marmalade

3. You find parents:
   A) in your house
   B) at the supermarket near the cold meat counter
   C) under the stairs in the damp corner

Answer "A" scores 2 points.
Answer "B" scores 1 point.
Answer "C" scores 0 points.

1

How did you do?
0-3 points: You definitely need this book, but you should learn to read first.

3-9 points: Well, you seem to know something about parents, but this book would certainly help you clear up any confusions. (It will also help you clear up any spilt coffee, as it is made of very absorbent paper.)

More than 9 points: You must have cheated! Buy the book anyway!

YOU'RE GOING TO HAVE TO BUY THE BOOK IN ANY CASE. NOBODY ELSE WILL WANT IT AFTER YOU'VE BEEN FIDDLING WITH IT!

WARNING!
This book is very very serious. Well, a bit serious, anyway. Well, not much. A little bit serious. Well, hardly serious at all. Actually, some of the words might *look* serious, but that's because they're very long ones. Well, quite long. Long-ish, but not very long. Hardly long at all, really. Quite short in fact. In some cases, seriously short, but not very serious. Quite funny, actually. In fact, very funny. Very very funny even . . .
You have been warned!!

Preface

Coping With Parents is the ultimate reference book on the subject of parents. Literally minutes of exhaustive (and exhausting) research have gone into its creation. But how did it all start?

Some of the finest brains in the country were gathered together, chopped, rolled in flour, lightly fried with onions and bacon to a crisp golden brown, turned out into a medium casserole dish, enriched with the addition of a cook-in sauce, and placed in a hot oven (gas mark 8) for 35 minutes, or until tender, then laid on a bed of boiled rice (serves four to six).

This was the meal given to a group of the world's top experts, and yet they still agreed to contribute to this book (after they had recovered). These experts were hand-picked (by sticking a pin in a telephone directory). All of them have either *been* parents or have *had* parents. All of them are men and women (and in at least one case both), who are outstanding in a particular field. That is to say, they are all homeless. So, naturally, the modest fee they will receive for their contribution to this fine work will go some way to putting a roof over their heads.

So, who are these experts? I was able to get a quick look at the labels in their St Michael vests, as they crouched in communion along the edge of my bath, wishing the meal many happy returns. This is research, something I am good at (the meal was "cooking", something I am bad at). The experts are:

Elderado Dingbatti

A fellow of the University of Chobham. Also a fellow of very strange habits, none of which need concern us now. Elderado was recently offered the English Chair at Kings College, Oxford. He turned it down, explaining that he had just ordered a complete set of tubular ones from MFI, but thank you very much anyway.

Sam "Fingers" Golightly

Sam was educated at the University of Life (believed to be a Pool Hall in Walthamstow). Sam is a great believer in the value of books. He discovered at a very early age that books could help him get what he wanted. For example, at the age of just four and a half, he discovered that seven books, placed one on top of the other, enabled him to reach the old biscuit barrel where his mother kept her house-keeping money. He also discovered many other interesting facts about books. For instance, the *Complete Works of Shakespeare* brought down sharply on the back of the average person's head will render them unconscious for 3.7 minutes, easily long enough to go through their pockets. Sam admits that he owes a great deal to books. He also owes a great deal to book*ies*. Sam finally over-reached himself by going into the Listening Bank and trying to obtain a new kind of bank account: one where you don't need a chequebook, or a chequecard. You just need a gun, a large sack, and a bank-teller who is prepared to fill up the large sack with money every time you point the gun at them. Sam eventually gave up his life of crime, when he realized that you didn't get a pension at the end of it.

Mr X

A well-known writer forced to assume an alias after saying, in an article in *The Sunday Times*, that the Archibishop of Canterbury had nice legs. He was threatened with being made to appear on the *Wogan* show. Fearing for his reputation, he took to wearing a Sainsbury's carrier bag on his head. When this wore out, realizing he could not obtain another without buying a large quantity of groceries, he had extensive (and expensive) plastic surgery. So much so, that he has recently had to give up sunbathing, in case he melts. I had to collect his contribution to the book from a hollow tree on Wimbledon Common. At the same time I also picked up a large envelope full of military secrets in the form of a Russian plan to invade Skegness. I also picked up several very nasty bites from a squirrel who thought I was trying to pinch his nuts (actually I did, but it was an accident). It was in fact Mr X who came up with the title for this book. Over a game of squash one day, which he lost due to the carrier bag, I told him that I was writing a book about coping with parents, but didn't know what to call it. Without a moment's hesitation he turned to me, and said: "Why not call it 'Coping With Parents'?"

I am indeed fortunate to have him on my team. At least I assume that he is still a "him". I'm not sure of the extent of the plastic surgery.

Anne Expert

Ms Expert is no stranger to controversy, although she is probably a total stranger to you. She has written over three hundred books, none of which have ever been published. Unfortunately this has not deterred her in any way. A keen supporter of causes, Ms Expert has been saving whales. She now has several, and can hardly get into her flat. She had hoped to become a social worker, but failed the entrance exam, by writing a thesis entitled "King Herod, the Children's Friend".

Professor A. Doctor

Archibald Doctor obtained his professorship by mail-order from a box number in Gwent. However, he is far from being an uneducated man (but not very far). He has twenty-seven "A" levels, all of them distinction passes in woodwork. This strange fact stems from his deep-seated love of coffee tables. Archie's major contribution to this book was his suggestion that I should try to get as much of the spelling correct as possible, as this would make it easier to read.

"Not for me it wouldn't," I ventured to point out. However, I believe that I owe him a debt of gratitude for his far-sightedness. I also apparently owe him £1.25 for his bottle of Tipp-Ex.

Eve-May Foskett (Mrs)

Not originally my choice as part of the carefully hand-
picked team of experts, but she proved herself to be a
Trojan. She also ate like a horse (actually I think that
should read "she also ate a horse", although the details of
that particular mealtime are a little sketchy, due to the
large quantities of homemade privet wine consumed that
evening). Her contribution came in the form of advice
such as:

   "You're not going to put that in, are you?"
   "That's rubbish for a start."
   "Etc."
She certainly kept me on my toes, particularly when she
was hoovering.

Robert the Dachshund

Again, not really intended as a member of my meticulously balanced team, but Robert took it upon himself to do some preliminary editing of the original draft of the book. He chose a totally unique method of doing this: the bits of the book he liked he ate. The rest he . . . er . . . relieved himself all over. Therefore I think it is probably safe to say that what remains of this book will:

(A) be of little or no use as dog food, and

(B) be unsuitable for holding too close to your nose.

THOSE ARE THE EXPERTS, HERE IS THE BOOK

Introduction

The first line of any book is the most important.
I read that somewhere. In a book, probably.

And that's what this is, a book. I mention that in case
you've never seen one before. But this is no ordinary
book.

Oh, no. It is a reference book, a work of fact, which
contains the answers to all your parental problems. I wish
there had been a book like this around when I was
young(er!). I would have given my right arm for a book
like this. In fact I would have given my right arm for any
book that could easily have been held in one hand. This is
one of my many regrets.

Another of my many regrets is that I didn't listen at
school. If I had done, I might have heard the teacher say,
"You're sixteen now. You can leave school, if you like."
Instead of which I sat there until I was 32. I might still be
sat there now, if they hadn't pulled the school down to
build a supermarket. Just think, if I had stayed sitting
there, I might be a check-out person by now! Ah, regrets!
My mother wanted me to be an accountant. I wonder

why? Had she wanted to be an accountant herself, do you think? Was she simply living out a secret ambition through me? She never showed any leaning towards accountancy. Oh, sure, she used to count things, such as socks on washing day, her blessings (which took less time than the socks), and the number of people sitting down to dinner, in case I or my brother had brought someone home with us by mistake. It's easily done. You're packing your satchel, you're in a hurry, you're stuffing everything in it, and there's this really small kid who sits next to you . . . but I digress. I should really begin at the beginning . . .

What Are Parents?

In order to solve a problem, we first have to identify it. So, what actually are parents? Well, most of the obvious reference works — the *Beano*, *Dandy*, *SchoolFriend*, *Dalton's Weekly* — failed to mention parents at all. Even *Parents* magazine seems to concentrate on children rather than parents. So, naturally, I resorted to the good old *English Dictionary*. First, I consulted the *Concise Oxford Dictionary*, only to discover that there were some pages missing. I think the dog must have been "editing" again (a quick sniff proved this to be the case). Then I turned to the *Little Oxford*, which is the size of a house. That offered the following:

"**Parent**: One who has begotten an offspring." I then looked up "begotten", and found:

"**Begotten**: past participle of Beget." Then:

"**Beget**: Give rise to."

Now, I already happen to know that an offspring is something to do with the suspension of a car, therefore, according to the *Little Oxford*, a parent is anyone who causes the suspension of a car to rise, which counts out my

13

Aunty Mabel, who always causes the suspension of the car to go down quite considerably. Feeling less than happy with this definition, I turned to the *Pocket Dictionary*, which is about five times larger than the *Little Oxford* (where do they get these names from?). The *Pocket* offered:

"**Parent**: A mother or father, an organism, a source."

So, according to them, a parent is anything from a mum to a bottle of ketchup. But I do think we're getting closer. Incidentally, the English-German dictionary offered:

"**Parents**: Eltern." How did he get into it? He's not even married any more, is he?

For further enlightenment, I turned to *The Pocket Book of Quotations*, which, incidentally, you'd be lucky to get on a snooker table, let alone in a pocket. There I found the following:

Samuel Butler (1835-1902) said: "Parents are the last people on earth who should have children."

Oscar Wilde (1854-1900) said: "Children begin by loving their parents. After a time they judge them. Rarely, if ever, do they forgive them." And there's more . . .

Confucius (c.551-479BC) he say: "It's hard to find a cat in a darkened room, especially when it's not there." Ah, well, that's Chinese philosophy for you. Very hard to digest, and half an hour later you want some more.

PUT DOWN THAT PHILOSOPHY, ITS TEA TIME..... AND SIT UP STRAIGHT!

So let's summarize. What have we actually found out about parents? Not a lot. But this much we know:

They tend to be older than you.

They come in pairs, as a general rule.

We have all got them. Someone once said, and it was probably me, "If you haven't had parents, you haven't lived."

Still confused? Well, perhaps it's time to call in an expert:

Your Questions Answered
with Anne Expert

"Worried of Wapping" writes:
"I arrived home from school the other day, which is not particularly unusual. But, no sooner was I through the door, than this person started asking me what time I called this. I didn't really understand the question. Then this other person, a woman I think, started tugging at my coat, saying that I wouldn't feel the benefit if I didn't take it off. Something else I didn't understand. I was then made to eat something. I'm not sure what. It had obviously been 'cooked from frozen', and I think it was still in the box. The two people stood and stared at me, nodding and smiling, the whole time I was eating — or attempting to. Does this mean that I've got parents?"

Anne Expert says:
"It could do. But there is a little test you can try. Suddenly say, 'Mum?' or 'Dad?', very casually to no one in particular. If these people are not your parents, then they will naturally assume that you are talking to an invisible friend, and find an excuse to leave the room. If, on the

16

other hand, they do reply (a simple 'Yes?' would be sufficient) then I think it is fair to assume that they are your parents, although they still may not be. Another simple, and far less foolproof, test is to try to find out their surname (that's the name they always ask you to put down *first* on forms, before your Christian names, just to confuse you). You'll find their surname on any official papers, driving licence, court summons, organ donor card etc., that they may have in their pockets (reading my leaflet 'Pickpocketing for Beginners' would come in handy here). If their surname is the same as yours, it could indicate that you are in some way related. Of course, this test is more reliable if your surname is something unusual. For example: *Something-Unusual*, as in *Wayne Something-Unusual*. But be careful, neither of these tests is particularly accurate (read my leaflet: 'Learning To Live With Burglars')."

A Doctor writes
"A great number of people come to me with their problems, which are many and various. But I always have the perfect solution. I tell them to drop their trousers. You see, four years of medical school, three years of university, two years of sixth-form college, a degree in biology and 27 woodwork A-levels have given me the unique ability to get straight to the bottom of things."

What Can I Do About Having Parents?

Well, the first thing I would say is this: don't panic.

As I mentioned previously, everyone has at some point had parents. So, you're not alone. Although I realize that it can seem that way. It can be very traumatic. As in the case of Derek. Derek is thirteen. He is very typical of a boy of his age. In fact, he is a typical thirteen-year-old. He has this to say:

"I realize now that I have had them all my life. But I never really noticed them until recently. I suppose, up until then, they hadn't really been a problem. But, suddenly, I've noticed people staring. Even when it's only one of them, like when we're out shopping for school clothes, etc, people still giggle and point. Of course, I know that everyone has got them, that I'm not some sort of freak, but it doesn't make it any easier to handle. I feel like turning round and shouting, 'Look at yours, then! At least mine are only little. Yours are huge and fat!'. But I know that this won't help. I mean, I've got them, and I'm just going to have to make the most of it."

Well done, Derek! He has the good sense to realize that

the problem won't go away (unless you change the locks while they're out). You are stuck with it. And, if you can accept that and come to terms with it, you are half-way to dealing with the problem in a rational and adult fashion. Sorry, that's a contradiction in terms. I mean a rational, unadult, fashion.

So, to summarize: recognize the problem; realize that everyone else has the same problem . . . AND DON'T PANIC!

A doctor writes
People often say to me: "Hallo, Doctor!"

Who Are These People?

I blame the media. The media projects an image of parents that we know to be totally false.

Try this simple test:

1. Night after night you come home from school, or paper-round, or whatever. Are you immediately invited to sit down to a cordon bleu meal, which your mother has spent the entire day preparing (with the help of a beef stock cube, of course)?
>   No.
>   Yes.
>   Erm.

(Tick your answer)

2. You need a bike. Any old bike will do. You mention this to your dad. Does he chuckle, tousle your hair and say "You don't want one of them daft racing bikes with the funny saddles!"? Does he then phone round the shops for the most expensive bike the world has ever

known, with drop handlebars, fifty-eight speed gears, turbo thrust, power assisted brakes and racing tyres?
No.
Yes.
Erm.

3. You get up in the morning. You feel very hungry. So, not unreasonably, you make yourself some Marmite toast. So, OK, you overdo it a bit. You actually make a mountain of the stuff — so big that Chris Bonnington phones up and asks if he can come round and conquer it. You realize what you've done and think that perhaps you'd better offer Mum some, in case she's cross. This is called "damage limitation", and makes perfect sense. Then your Mum sees the mountain of toast. Does she smile, chuckle and give you a cuddle?
No.
Yes.
Erm.

4. You are indulging in a bit of "horse-play" with your father, and you inadvertently dislocate his shoulder. Does he immediately take you out and buy you a Big Mac?

No.
Yes.
Erm.

5. You come home covered in mud. Not your fault, of course. You were pushed. Does your mother give a long-suffering but indulgent smile, and then set about getting your clothes so white that they glow in the dark and have to be tested for radiation?

No.
Yes.
Erm.

How Did You Do?

Five "No's": Well done. You're on the way to getting cured.

Five "Yes's": Oh dear! You're still on the danger list!

Five "Erm's": Am I using too many long words for you?

You see, none of the so-called parents featured in these situations are actually real. They're actors dressed up as human beings. I mean, I've seen that Oxo Mum on Blanketty Blank. If she was really cooking all those meals, she wouldn't have time to appear on the telly in *adverts*, let alone game shows. You see, these parents are media images of parents, and not to be believed. Like most things dreamed up by the media, they are about as far from real life as Gillingham are from winning the FA Cup. Mind you, that's the media for you. You should never believe anything you read in the papers. Except, of course, anything under a headline like:

"Popstar Ate My Gerbil!"

"My Mother-in-Law was a Sofa-Bed!"

"Aliens Abducted my Wife!"

"I Married my Own Golf-Clubs!"

Everything like that is obviously completely true. I mean, no one could make up things like that, could they?

But parents are different. Different from anything else you'll ever encounter (except possibly Russell Grant). And this is why they are so unpredictable, and difficult to cope with. After all, in order to cope with something, you have to be able to stay one step ahead. But how do you stay one step ahead of something which has a thought process that is more complex and more illogical than the bylaws of the local park? I can't understand those at all. They all seem to be about dogs fouling and not playing football.

When I was younger, I couldn't really see how a dog could commit a foul, if he wasn't playing football in the first place. Then it was pointed out to me exactly what "dog fouling" meant. After that I couldn't understand why footballers got sent off for fouling on the pitch, when I for one hadn't seen them do it. No wonder people are always saying that the referee needs glasses. Anyway . . .

How do parents get like they do? Are they born like it? No.

So what turns a perfectly sane, friendly, easy-going adult (well, as sane, friendly and easy-going as an adult ever gets) into an irrational freak? I sent my team of experts out into the field with packed lunches and instructions not to come back. Or, at least, not to come back until they had the answer to the question. Unfortunately I forgot to tell them the question, and so they still haven't returned. They'll be back soon. It's getting dark, and none of them is fluorescent. But . . .

What Makes a Parent?

According to my research, or rather the conversation I had with the woman next door as I videotaped her hanging out her washing. At least, I assume it was hers. It may not have been. I confess that I've never seen her wear any of it, but then she always seems to be in that diving suit whenever I see her. Strange woman. A parent, of course. But, apparently, it all starts with a conversation that goes something like this:

She: (*putting her arms round his neck*) Darling . . .

He: I've already given you £300 this week.

She: No, darling. Not that. I've got a surprise for you.

He: I don't like the sound of that. Don't tell me . . . the mortgage has gone up.

She: No. well . . . yes. But it's not that either.

He: You've scratched my Rolf Harris's Greatest Hits album.

She: No. No. Look at me. Do I look different?

He: Well, yes. You do. I know, you're wearing a new skirt!

She: No.

He: You're wearing a new blouse!

She: No!

He: You're wearing a gas mask?

She: No! Listen. What would you say if I told you that we're soon going to hear the patter of tiny feet?

He: I'd say: "Oh, no!"

She: Why?

He: Because last time we heard the patter of tiny feet, Martians had landed in the back garden. I phoned the council, but did they do anything about it? Of course not. Those Martians completely took over my greenhouse. God alone knows what they did in there, but we've not had a decent crop of tomatoes since. If I hadn't offered them your mother for experimentation, I think we would have never got rid of them. They'd still be in there, throwing their all-night pyjama and Tupperware parties, and trying to phone Patrick Moore on the garden hose.

She: Oh, don't get on your hobby-horse!

He: How can I? We put it in the attic. shortly after we decided that we didn't want children.

She: Well, I think we might have to get it down again.

He: Get it down? Not on your life. If you think I'm crawling around in the attic and humping around a flaming great rocking horse, with my back the way it is, is, just because a load of flipping Martians have turned up uninvited on the patio, you've got another think coming.

She: Oh, don't start that!

He: Start what?

She: Whenever I try to have a conversation, you start talking to me in very long sentences with hardly any punctuation.

He: Don't!

She: You do! Then you do that.

He: What?

She: Go all monosyllabic on me.

He: Don't!

She: Do!

He: Don't!

She: Do!

etc . . . etc . . .

And so it goes on. Eventually she is able to break the news that she is going to become a Mummy. Which probably means that he is going to become a Daddy. And this is when the change starts.

She starts eating for two. Soon she has to stop buying her clothes at Woman at C & A . . .

And start going to . . . Rent-a-Tent at Milletts.

He starts drinking for two. This is known as "wetting the baby's head", and actually isn't supposed to happen until the day of the baby's birth. However, it does require practice in order to get it right . . .

I'M AS PRACTISED AS A NEWT

"Wetting the baby's head": that's a stupid expression, isn't it? I mean, how can a bunch of blokes having a drink in a pub possibly wet a baby's head? Anyway, those of you who have been roped in to change your baby brother's nappy will already know that a baby can wet it's own head with amazing accuracy. It can also include the wall, you, the clean clothes you've just laid out for it, and almost the whole of the rest of the room in its aim. The mobiles can be dripping for months. So it doesn't need any help from a bunch of wallies in a pub.

What sex will it be?
This is the next thing that occupies the days and nights of the would-be parent. Parents are often heard to say, "I don't mind what it is as long as it's healthy." Do they seriously expect anyone to believe that?

Of course there are ways for parents to tell the sex of the child. Here is one of them:

Suspend a gold ring on a piece of cotton over the expectant mother's tummy, and observe the movements of the ring. If the ring goes from side to side, this means that the baby could be a boy, but it might be a girl. If the ring goes in circles, this means that the baby could be a girl, but it might be a boy.

This test is not very accurate.

Another not very accurate test is for the would-be-mother to look at the screen when she goes to hospital for the check-up scan. Unfortunately the picture on the monitor is often rather like watching satellite TV without a dish.

The most accurate way of telling the sex of a child is to wait until it's born, and look. Mind you, you do have to know what you're looking for . . .

What will we call it?

Another thing that occupies parents' thoughts is what they will call their child once it arrives. After all, there are so many names to choose from. At one time, children got named after saints. Lots of girls were called Mary, Theresa, Joan, etc. Boys tended to be called after the names of the Apostles and disciples: Mark, Matthew, Luke, John, Thomas, Simon, etc. Not surprisingly, very few boys got called Judas! This custom has expanded to include monarchs (Elizabeth, Victoria, George) and famous people. In particular, popular film stars and pop stars of the day. That was fine when pop stars were called things like Cliff, but imagine being lumbered with a name like Elton, or Sting, or Bono. Bono Johnson. No, it's a bit of a handful, isn't it? Still, I suppose it's better than being called Bros Wilson, or Violet Femmes Higginbottom.

But, as we've already established, parents don't think. If did, they would find out what the name *meant* before lumbering their unsuspecting child with it. My name, Peter, means "like a rock". But that could suggest that I'm as Thick as a Brick, couldn't it? But I'm not. Well, OK, maybe just a small stone. Then there's KEVIN. Now Kevin means gentle, kind and loveable. Which is nice to know. It must be quite a comfort to know that you're gentle, kind and loveable, even if you have got a silly name, mustn't it? Mind you, Kevin isn't the silliest name I came across in my research (well, not quite!). There's JABEZ, for example. It means "Cause of Sorrow", which is hardly surprising really, is it? I mean, I think I'd have cause to be sad if I was called Jabez. KEN, by the way, means "Clear as water". In other words — a drip!

Then there's ANGELA. A hard name to live up to, because it means "The Bringer of Good News":

> **YOU**: Hello, Angela. What are you doing here?
> **ANGELA**: I just came to tell you that your hamster's dead. Bye.

Then there's ADRIAN — "The Man of the Sea". So why does he nearly drown every time he has a wash?
BARRY — "Spearlike, sharp intellect". So why hasn't he got any "O" levels?
BRIAN — "Powerful strength". So why do the big kids keep thumping him?
DEREK — "Ruler of the people". So why have there never been any Kings called Derek? Mind you, DON means "Ruler of the world", and there hasn't been a World Ruler, has there? Not even one called Don. Although Mafia Godfathers are all called Don, which is odd because they are all Italians. But what about more

32

modern names? WAYNE, for example, means "Wagon Maker", although I suppose nowadays that could be interpreted as "Used Car Salesman". Then there's SHANE, which is actually a version of John. JOHN means "God's Gracious Gift". I must tell my brother that. He's called John, but I doubt that he knows that he's supposed to be a precious gift, somehow!

TRACEY — "Battler". That's fine if she's built like Frank Bruno.

STACEY — "She who will rise again". Not a lot of use if she's no good at getting up in the morning!

All this is fairly conclusive proof, if proof were needed, that parents simply do not know what they are doing when it comes to choosing names. So . . .

Why do they do it?

The main reason that parents spend so much effort thinking of names, planning for their child, etc, is to fill in time. After all, they have to wait nine months for your arrival, what else can they do? Imagine it. Waiting nine months for something you want very much. Could you do that? Would you like it if you went into a shop and all you wanted was a bag of sweets, but you had to wait nine months for delivery? No, of course not. So perhaps some of this behaviour is understandable. Or, at least, it would be if it stopped there. But it doesn't . . .

After the birth

If you think parents behave badly before you're born (not that you'd know much about it at the time, of course), they behave much worse after the happy event. They monitor your every movement. They disclose your most intimate details to total strangers. In fact, years later you could be introduced to some important person, who floors you by saying, "Oh, yes! Your father's told me *all about you*!" But worst of all, they photograph absolutely everything. And I do mean everything. This is when you curse progress. Time was when operating a camera was beyond the reach of your average person. Now, they are so totally idiot-proof that even an adult can work one. And all these secrets go into the . . .

Baby Book

BABY'S FIRST
STOOL

BABY'S FIRST
MOVEMENT

BABY'S FIRST
STAND

CUSTER'S LAST
STAND

Now, of course, there is nothing wrong with parents having a record of your childhood. It gives them something to do when they're old and grey and none of their friends talk to them any more. But why do they assume that all your friends will be interested in seeing the secrets of your (often sordid) past? Why are prospective boyfriends or girlfriends subjected to a private viewing every time they come within two hundred miles of your house?

This is just another example of the madness that grips ordinary people when they become parents. But what causes it? I'll tell you. It's a little thing called: PARENTHOOD.

I will explain exactly what this is in the next chapter.

A doctor writes
"After many years of practicing as a doctor, I am beginning to wonder if I'll ever get good enough to stop practicing and do it properly!"

What Is Parenthood?

A parenthood is a special hat or cap, worn by the parent. Down the centuries the design has changed of course. Here are some examples. As you can see, there have been a variety of types, but they all have one thing in common. They are very tight and uncomfortable. This naturally affects the brain and causes the wearer to behave in a strange manner. Today, thanks to modern technology (or, in fact, no thanks to modern technology), the parenthood is completely invisible. But the effects are exactly the same. Once the parenthood has been put on, it cannot ever be taken off again. This may go some way to explain the wearer's strange behaviour. But, although you may well be relieved to discover the cause of your particular parents' irrational attitudes, this knowledge does not in fact do a great deal to help you cope with the situation.

Over the next few chapters I hope to resolve this problem.

NORMAN PARENTHOOD

ITALIAN PARENTHOOD

FRENCH PARENTHOOD

TUDOR PARENTHOOD

POST-WAR PARENTHOOD

Understanding the Problem

So. We've established that parental lunacy is mainly caused by an invisible hat. But how does this madness manifest itself? There are, of course, a variety of different ways. Some of them subtle, some less so. One of the more obvious ways that springs to mind is the fact that they ask questions to which they already know the answer. I imagine you will have noticed this. Questions such as:

"Have you tidied your room?"

"Have you fed your gerbil?"

"Would you like to go shopping for a nice new school mac?"

"Have you done your homework?"

"Have you cleaned your bike?"

"Would you like to run an errand for me?"

"Would you like to go to Grandma's?"

And, of course:

"What time do you call this?"

They also develop the ability to say things that mean something completely different. For example:

Phrase	Meaning
Wait until your birthday	You'll have forgotten by then
Don't answer back	You're right and I'm wrong
Wait till your father gets home	I'm passing the buck
Ask your Mother	I'm passing the buck as well
Where does your friend live?	He/she looks a bit common to me
Would you like sauce with your meal?	I know it's revolting, but it's all there is
Don't you want to go on the school trip?	Damn! We were going to move while you were away!

Another symptom of this parenthood madness is the way they say things that don't make sense. Like:

"Work hard at school, and the world could be your oyster."

Have you ever seen an oyster? It's a sort of grubby shell thing, with a lid that is almost impossible to get off. When you do finally manage it, you find something that looks like a large bogey. Try to eat it, and you'll find it very tough to chew and very salty. Come to think of it, it probably *is* a bogey! Is that the extent of your parents' ambitions for you? That they want you to work hard so that your entire future can revolve around a large bogey? Some ambition, eh?

Why are parents so obsessed with your future, anyway? What does it matter to them what job you finally end up doing? Do they want to come and watch you at work, or something? Actually, watching people working is something that we in Britain seem to find very fascinating.

I don't know if you've ever noticed, but on building sites they put a solid wooden screen around the site, so that you can't see them, then they put little windows in the screen, so that you *can* see them. Pretty soon a decent sized crowd arrives, certainly as large as the average crowd at Aldershot football ground on a typical Saturday (five old men and a dog). But I don't somehow think that this is why your parents get so interested in your future prospects. But they definitely do.

From the first days of your life every action is interpreted as an indication of your future vocation. Kick your legs a lot, and your Dad says, "He (or even "She's") going to be a footballer!" Gurgle a lot, and you're going to be a singer. Even a kid who picks his nose is put down as a potential brain surgeon. It's strange, isn't it? No parent ever thinks that their child has the makings of a great dustman, or a brilliant lorry-driver. No parent ever looks at their newborn babe and proudly declares: "He's going to be a layabout, you can tell." Which is odd, because that's what most babies are really good at — laying about. So why do they do it? Why do they get obsessions about your future? The answer's simple, and it has little or nothing to do with the invisible hat. But it has everything to do with boasting. Yes. Boasting. They want to boast. They want to be able to say, "My son the brain surgeon", or "My daughter the Prime Minister". They have little or no desire to say, "My son the unemployed, unqualified layabout", even if that's what you are. Of course, they have to be careful. Different jobs are more (or less) acceptable in different parts of the country. For instance, the parent who starts boasting that his son is a dustman in, say, Weybridge, is going to get looked down on (particularly if they are not very tall). But, by the same token, your mum will get funny looks if she tells the inhabitants of Glasgow that you are a ballet dancer. So, it's very much "horses for courses", or at least it is in Epsom, Cheltenham and Aintree.

The following may help to illustrate my point more clearly. Use the key below to see which jobs are acceptable in which parts of the country:

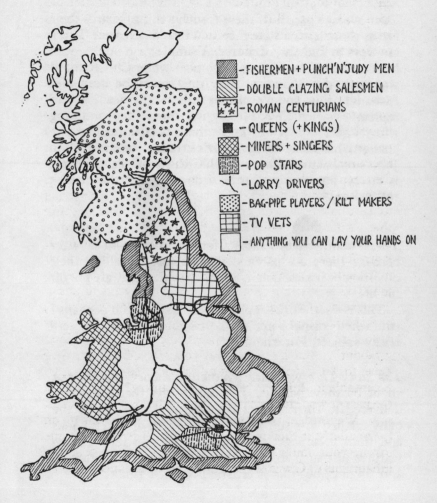

- FISHERMEN + PUNCH 'N' JUDY MEN
- DOUBLE GLAZING SALESMEN
- ROMAN CENTURIANS
- QUEENS (+KINGS)
- MINERS + SINGERS
- POP STARS
- LORRY DRIVERS
- BAG-PIPE PLAYERS / KILT MAKERS
- TV VETS
- ANYTHING YOU CAN LAY YOUR HANDS ON

Taboo topics

In what other ways does this madness manifest itself? Well, there are several subjects that parents flatly refuse to discuss.

Age:
Your average parent (if there is such a thing) guards their age as though it's a state secret. Why? Who cares? There are ways to find out, of course. A simple yard-stick would be something like: if they remember when Cliff Richard was with the Shadows, then they must be very old. Although this doesn't always follow. I mean, I can remember when Elvis Presley was called Reg, and sang with "The Trogs", but I'm not that old. (I wonder why he changed his name to Elvis? It's strange, because Elton John's real name is Reg, as well. Cliff Richard's real name is Harry, apparently. But how do we know that it isn't really Reg?)

Sex:
This is another taboo subject for most parents. I say *most* because there are parents who delight in telling their offspring every last detail. So much so that they are put off for life!

This is not the time or place to discuss sex, but perhaps I could help dispel some of the rumours about this very tricky subject. For example:

The Stork Theory: Clearly a ludicrous theory, but one put about by some parents. The theory says that babies are delivered to their mother by a stork, which carries the baby cradled in a soft white cloth. There are even books and films to support this theory. Walt Disney's *Dumbo* features just such an event. He even has the stork talking and singing, but that is artistic licence, I think.

One look at the average stork will tell you that this theory is a complete non-starter. A newborn baby can weigh anything up to around ten pounds. That's equivalent to five bags of sugar. All the storks I've ever seen have to really struggle to pick up an average-sized fish, let alone a shelf-load of Tate & Lyle. And even if they managed to get off the ground, how would they land? Have you seen their legs? Like twigs, they are. One false landing and they'd snap clean off.

OK. Supposing by some trick of nature, a stork is able to both fly and land carrying a large infant. How does it actually deliver the baby to the mother? Through the window? What if nobody left the window open? Perhaps this clever little stork unlatches the window with its left buttock (do stork have left buttocks? I don't know). In front of all those doctors and nurses? Have you ever heard a doctor say, "Hello. I'm Doctor Wilson. I opened the window for the stork that delivered your baby brother." No. Of course not. Mind you, no doctor worth his salt is actually going to admit that he spent four years at medical school, and got half the alphabet after his name, only to wind up specializing in opening windows for storks, is he?

No. Personally I think the stork theory is a complete wash-out. Then, of course, there's . . .

43

The Gooseberry Bush Theory: This theory suggests that babies are found under gooseberry bushes. Have you ever seen a gooseberry bush? There probably wouldn't be a problem getting the baby under there. But, given the average birth-rate virtually anywhere in the world, half the plant-life on this planet would have to be gooseberry bushes, in order to accommodate the babies. I don't ever recall seeing *one* gooseberry bush, let alone millions. Maybe there's a special island somewhere, covered in gooseberry bushes, and all the babies are flown in from there. By stork. That's nearly as ludicrous as the idea that all parents wear a special invisible hat. Oh. Sorry. Did you believe that bit? Sorry! I'm afraid I made it up.

That's another thing parents do — lie to you. For example: some of the time they say that there *is* a Father Christmas, and some of the time they say that there *isn't*. Well, you don't have to be a genius to work out that this means that some of the time they are lying, and some of the time they are telling the truth. The trick is to work out which is which.

Friends:
This is something else that parents have a strange attitude towards. I mean, why should they assume that they need to help you select your friends? You don't help them to select theirs, do you? Perhaps you should. After all, have you seen some of their friends? You wouldn't be seen dead with most of them, would you? Although some of them look as though they might already be in that state. There's that friend of your dad's, who appears to come round only in order to fall asleep in the chair. Maybe he hasn't got any furniture at his own house. Maybe he hasn't even got a house. Judging from his hair he probably lives in a bush. Then there's the friend of your mum's from work that your dad nearly married but then married your mum

instead. That was a narrow escape — for somebody! Of course there's also the bloke who looks a bit like Bernard Manning and only knows one joke, a bit like Bernard Manning.

But do you say anything? Of course not! It would be impolite. But your parents don't seem to realize that. They seem to think it's perfectly OK to discuss your friends in front of them, as though they're deaf, or mad or something. Why?

Did they object to your friends when you were younger? Not really. In fact they seemed rather fond of your best friend "Binky", even though Binky was invisible, wore a magic hat and lived in the toilet. But the same cannot be said for your pal from school, who doesn't wear a magic hat, or live in the toilet (in fact he very rarely goes anywhere near any part of the bathroom). And he is certainly visible. In fact, you couldn't miss him. He's extremely visible, and verbal, not to mention occasionally aromatic. But a thoroughly nice sort, for all that. Do your parents like him? Of course not! And they hardly know him! It all seems very unfair!

Money:
When you were younger, your parents seemed to be continually buying you things — ice-creams, sweets, all the things in fact that they now seem to have decided are really bad for you. (Though not apparently bad for your younger brother, who eats so many sweets that he's very nearly the size of Cornwall.) But now that you're older you've got a little part-time job, paper round, whatever. OK, so it doesn't bring you in a fortune, it isn't going to make you a millionaire, but it helps pay for the little important things of life: tapes, clothes, etc. But do your parents let you spend your money on these thing? No! They want you to save it. What for? A rainy day! When did

we last have a rainy day? Yesterday, wasn't it?

"Oh, good!" you thought to yourself. "A rainy day! Now I can spend some of my own money." But were you allowed to? Of course not! You even had to threaten your mum with a visit from Freddy Kreuger (the scourge of *Elm Street*), and whistle the *Jaws* theme while your dad was sat on the loo, in order to frighten them into letting you shell out for this book. And that's another thing . . .

Books:

The average parent would not mind you splashing out your hard-earned dosh on *Five Go to the Library*, *Noddy Builds a Wardrobe*, or *The Young Person's Guide to Macramé*, oh no! But come home the proud owner of *The Monster Book of Bogey Jokes* or *Five Billion Things to Do with a Dead Pigeon*, and you'll never hear the last of it. The same goes for . . .

Films, Videos and TV Shows:

Obviously there are plenty of things on TV that parents feel, quite rightly, will corrupt their darling offspring. Programmes like *Bob Says Opportunity Knocks*, *Catchphrase* and *Emmerdale Farm*, for example. But do they video these dangerous items, to be viewed later behind a locked door? Of course not. Do they even turn them off, so that their poor little children's minds won't be tainted? No! They send you out of the room, lock you under the stairs, or sellotape a soundproof carrier bag over your head. Anything rather than turn the TV off. I'm convinced that many parents don't even know where the "Off" button is. They probably think that all TVs are turned off in London by the bloke who reads the late-night news. He pulls the plug out before he goes home, or something. Except that TV is on all night now, isn't it? That's probably only because

even *they* can't decide whose job it is to turn it off.

I suppose you could take the responsibility in your house for turning the set off when there was nothing worth watching. But then you'd only get into trouble for fiddling with something that didn't belong to you, wouldn't you? You can't win, really, can you? Its like . . .

School:

Now, most parents are only too willing to admit that they really hated school. And, yet, they tell you that it's good for you. How can this be? How can anything that makes you unhappy, sick, bored and depressed be good for you? Sure, evil-tasting medicine is probably good for you, because, although it's absolutely foul, it makes you better. But the same cannot be said of school.

47

I managed to find an old diary of mine, written when I was a mere schoolboy. Of course, it dates back to the sixties. (Well, fifties-sixties!), so it's more or less an antique. Here is a typical week:

MONDAY APRIL 5th

Lively start to the week. We were all called into the hall to watch a public hanging of one of the first years who had forgotten his games kit. Unfortunately his head came off, but, so as not to waste it, we later used it as the ball in a match against the local Grammar School. We won 57-0, after all of their side had been sent off for setting fire to one of the linesmen. The game was rather held up while the pitch was redeveloped and a high rise block of flats was built, but this delay was added on at the end, so we played three minutes' extra time (*The flats were condemned the following day, but are still inhabited to this day*). Had cabbage for school dinner.

TUESDAY APRIL 6th

Double woodwork today. Hurray! We all made a towel holder. Mine looked almost like one. I really feel that I'm making progress. I've only been doing woodwork for six years, and already I can make a towel holder. Teacher is so impressed that next week he said that some of us can have a go at making a doorstop. That's really difficult, apparently. Fairly boring day apart from that. Four teachers had nervous breakdowns, but that's nothing new. Had cabbage for school dinner.

WEDNESDAY APRIL 7th

When we got to school, we all found (or at least, those of us who can count found) that four classrooms had been stolen. They think it was an ex-pupil who was carrying a grudge. That's stupid. How could anyone carry a grudge *and* four classrooms? He must be very

48

strong, that's all I can say. To overcome the shortage of classrooms, we moved some benches outside and had our lessons out there. It wasn't snowing that much. We did Egyptian history, and had great fun embalming a really spotty kid who had arrived with a note for Miss. It turned out to be a love letter from the new PE teacher, who's very good looking, according to some of the girls (and a few of the boys). Anyway, they had obviously arranged to meet at dinner time, because some of our class followed them and made kissing noises. I didn't. I didn't want to miss cabbage.

THURSDAY APRIL 8th

Biology. We were doing the Facts of Life, but then the teacher turned up, so we had to stop. At first it looked like it was going to be a waste of a lesson, because we couldn't find anything to dissect. Fortunately Jenkins had his cat with him, so that was OK. Firstly we did an experiment called: "Is The Book Cupboard Large enough To Swing A Cat In?" It wasn't. But at least it meant that the cat didn't feel it when we dissected him (I think it was a him. I didn't get that bit to dissect). Most of us had cabbage for lunch. Jenkins didn't. He said it was *his* cat, so he could do what he wanted with it.

FRIDAY APRIL 9th

Jenkins wasn't in school today. He should have stuck to the cabbage. The rest of us did (*I still can't get it off my teeth, all these years later*). At least you can be sure that the cabbage has been cooked long enough. They boil up enough at the weekend to last the week (*I've since discovered that this isn't exactly true. They actually used to boil up enough over the summer holidays to last the whole of the school year*). The end of another week. Some of us don't want to go home for the weekend.

Some of us can't. Especially those who are chained to their desks. Someone has hidden the hacksaw.

As you can see, a very typical school week. Hardly anything has changed over the years. Certainly nothing to write home about, those of us who can write. And yet parents are obsessed with you going to school.

Fashion:
Most parents are also obsessed with what you wear. Why? They say things like: "I don't want to be seen with you dressed like that!" But surely that's fine! You don't want them to be seen with *you* dressed like that. In fact, you don't really want them to be seen with you at all! Parents worry about what their friends will say when they see you. But they also say things like:
    "You look like someone else. Not like my little girl/boy at all."
But, if you don't look anything like yourself, how are their friends going to recognize you? So, what does it matter what you look like, if no one knows who you are?

Parents say: "We didn't go around dressed like that when we were your age!" Which is true, more or less. But what *did* they go around dressed like, eh? Ask them that!

Unfortunately (or fortunately for them), most family photo albums record such events as weddings, christenings, the cat's operation, and so forth. So they give the impression that your parents, grandparents, aunts and uncles spent their entire lives dressed in suits and standing in rows, grinning like lunatics (or in the case of the cat's operation, dressed in white coats, holding kitchen knives and wondering what to do next). But that was, of course, not the case. Yes — that balding chap you call Dad, the one over there in the Marks and Spencer zip-up cardigan with the little suede shoulder patches, he was once a Fashion Slave! He was! Hard to believe, isn't it? Even harder to imagine him, as he is now, looking like he did then.

And what about Mum? She too could have been, in the words of the well-known song by the Kinks (what well-known song by the Kinks?), A Dedicated Follower of Fashion. (Oh, that well-known song by the Kinks! Who *are* the Kinks?)

Depending on their age (which we've already established parents refuse to discuss) they could be wearing any of the natty little fashion items on the next page, and listening to music ranging from the New Seekers, Peter and Gordon, to the Beatles. (Oh, by the way, I felt very old one day when, in a record shop I saw a girl looking at a Beatles' album, and saying, "Oh, I didn't realize that Paul McCartney had been in a group before Wings!" Those of you who are now saying, "Who are Wings?" are making me feel even older!)

Then of course there was Sham 69, the Clash, the Sex Pistols (I said I wouldn't discuss sex, didn't I?), and Rolf Harris. Rolf Harris had a huge hit with "Two Little Boys". I can't remember *their* names.

A lot of parents in the sixties and seventies called their children things like "Starburst", "Sunchild" and "Rainbow". These poor people are adults now. Parents even. Imagine being stuck with a name like Rainbow Higginbottom. No wonder some parents are cagey about their names! But, just because *their* parents gave *them* a naff name, it doesn't justify them lumbering you with something like Kevin! Especially if you're a girl!

There are, of course, many other ways in which parents behave strangely, or express strange attitudes. Like their attitude towards bed, for instance. They are continually trying to make you go to bed: you need your sleep, etc., etc. Then, at an all-night party, when obviously everyone gets very tired, you discover that the bedroom doors are locked! Weird! You can't even get your coat! Yet another example of the weird and wonderful world of parents.

But what can one do?

Nothing. They are the way they are. Being a parent is not, as yet, a recognized medical condition. And, considering the way the Health Service is going, I can't see that it ever will be. So it's just something that one has to live with, I'm afraid. It's not terminal (which means that you can't catch buses from it), so that's something at least.

Not much, but something. I suppose one source of comfort is the fact that some people who were born with parents have gone on to become quite famous, and achieve great things. Hitler, for instance. Actually, I think he's probably a bad example. Alright, Bros — they're good examples. What of, I'm not too sure! However, many people have survived having parents and discovered things, like penicillin, invented things like the telephone, made things like money, and conquered things like countries. But . . .

How Did They Do It?

Christopher Columbus (1451-1506)
Columbus was a Spanish explorer who discovered America. Or rather, The Americas, as there were a few of them in those days. But, strange though it may seem, all the time he was discovering The Americas, he thought he was in China. Isn't that strange? Strange but true. Who sent him, and how did they react when he returned home?

FUNNY, HE DIDN'T LOOK CHINESE

Christopher Columbus: I'm home!

Mum: What time do you call this? I've been waiting for hours. Your dad's gone bull-fighting. He got bored.

Chris: Hope he doesn't get gored as well! Ha! Ha!

Mum: This is no time for jokes! I sent you out for a Chinese takeaway. Where is it?

Chris: I couldn't find one.

Mum: You couldn't . . . you must be dafter than you look, if that's possible! Honestly, call yourself an explorer! You should have become an accountant like I wanted. I knew it was a mistake to let you give up Maths! I don't know! Geography GCSE, and he can't even get a takeaway for all the tea in China!

Chris: I couldn't get tea, either. I just didn't find a restaurant.

Mum: Pathetic! Well, I'm starving!

Chris: I could have got you an Indian. The place was crawling with them.

Alexander Graham Bell (1847-1922)

Bell was the man who invented the telephone. He was researching deafness at the time. He was also trying to invent the record player, but Edison beat him to it. Did his parents care when he arrived home unexpectedly one day?

A G: Hello Mum. Dad.

Dad: Eh?

Mum: Oh, it's you. Hello, stranger.

A G: Yes, I know. I'm sorry I haven't written for a while . . .

Mum: We thought you'd broken both your arms, didn't we, Pop?

Dad: Eh?

Mum: (*shouting*) I said, we thought he'd . . . oh, never mind!

A G: Yes. I'm sorry. I really am. But I've been inventing the telephone.

Mum: Telephone! What do you need a telephone for? It's too much trouble for you to write, let alone pick up the telephone! Telephone — ha! (*Pause*) What *is* a telephone, anyway?

A G: It's something you talk to people with.

Mum: You mean "mouth". That's called a mouth! No point in inventing one of those! Everybody's already got one!

Dad: Eh?

Mum: I always said that expensive education of yours was a waste of time, didn't I, Pop?

Dad: Eh?

Mum: (*shouting*) I said I always said that . . . oh, never mind! Let's have a record on. I bet that Edison is good to his mother.

Dad: Eh?

King Harold II (c. 1022-66)

As Harold prepared for the Battle of Hastings, did he get some last-minute parental advice from his Mum?

HAVE YOU CLEANED YOUR TEETH?

Mum: Have you got your sandwiches?

Harold: Sandwiches? Listen, Mum, I don't think it's going to be that long a battle.

Mum: You never know! Better safe than sorry!

Harold: Well, if we need some, I'll send someone to Sandwich to get some. It's only up the road.

Mum: What about the flask I did for you?

Harold: Oh, Mum! Don't fuss!

Mum: It gets very chilly hanging about on them beaches. You know that Norman. He's always late. Look at the state of this chain-mail. (*Starts tugging at it*).

Harold: (*squirming*) Ooorr Muuuummm!

Mum: I wish you'd told me you'd got a battle on. I'd have given this lot a polish. Look at your tabard! That could do with an iron! Honestly, you might talk like someone off the council estate, no need to look like one as well!

(*Buglers heard outside*)

Harold: Look. I've got to go. The others are waiting.

Mum: That lot! They're no better than they should be, either! (*Hugs Harold*) Come here! Give your old Mum a kiss then. And tell those archers to be careful. They'll have somebody's eye out, one of these days.

Henry VIII (1491-1547)

Henry VIII married six times, which could easily have provoked the following reaction from his mother.

Mum: (*on the phone*) Henry? It's your mother. No, don't ring off. Henry . . . it's about your wife . . . What do you mean, which one? The present one, Anne . . . sorry to hear that. Who is it now? Jane Seymour? Oh. Very nice. Yes, dear. She is very attractive. I saw her the other night in a Bond film with that Roger Moore . . . you know, Thomas's little boy. What, dear? Of course I don't mind you getting married. It just surprises me that you need to do it so often. I mean no one can be *that* fond of wedding cake. And think of the cost. The photos, the food. all those awful relatives. Yes, dear. I know that there aren't that many relatives any more, but that's only because you keep chopping their heads off. You keep chopping your wives' heads off, too. It's hardly surprising that they've always got a headache!

John Logie Baird (1888-1946)

Baird developed the television (so it's his fault!). You can imagine his parents' reaction to his research.

Dad: (*opening the bedroom door*) Ah! There you are, John! It's time you and I had a little talk, man to man! Have you done your homework?

(*No reaction*)

Dad: I thought as much! You'll never make anything of yourself, you know! You're shiftless! Idle! A loafer! If you want to get on in this world, my boy, you've got to get out there! It's no good staring at that "box" day in day out.

Michelangelo (1475-1564)

Michelangelo was a famous Italian painter, who spent four years painting the ceiling of the Sistine Chapel in the Vatican. What would his parents have made of that?

Mum: (*as Michelangelo steps through the front door*) Stop! Don't you dare trail those dirty painty feet through on my nice clean carpet! I've only just this minute hoovered! Well . . . and where have you been till this time? I suppose you know your dinner's ruined? And your ice-cream's melted.

Michelangelo: I've been at the Sistine Chapel, Mother.

Mum: You're not still doing the Pope's ceiling, are you? Four years it's taken you! What's he having — Artex? Your Dad could have wallpapered the entire Vatican the time its taken you. That's if he hadn't got his trouble, that is. (*To Dad*) Couldn't you?

Dad: Course I could! (*To Michelangelo*) What are you doing it in, for Gawd's sake?

Michelangelo: Cherubs.

Dad: What's that? Matt or gloss?

Michelangelo: Flight of angels.

Dad: Sounds a bit poncy to me.

Mum: Yes! And meantime, if I want a lick o' paint on the fence I can go and whistle, I suppose! You've been promising to put a plug on the toaster for I don't know how long!

Michelangelo: This work is a calling.

Mum: I thought you said it was a ceiling!

Dad: A calling, is it? Yeah! Well, I know what they're calling you!

Mum: What you going to do if the Pope changes his mind when you've finished. He's not infallible, you know.

Michelangelo: I'll have finished soon. I just don't know what to use as the centrepiece.

Mum: Yes. Well. That's the last supper I'm cooking for you!

Michelangelo: (*suddenly inspired*) That's it! (*He starts to rush out*)

Dad: Now where are you off to?

Michelangelo: I can't stop.

Mum: Yes. Well, one thing before you go.

Michelangelo: Yes?

Mum: We think you're spending too much time with that boy David. People'll talk.

The A-Z of Parents

So far we have established that parents are strange, with an incurable, though not fatal, lunacy (not really brought on by the wearing of an invisible hat). We have also established that it is almost impossible to do anything other than grin and bear their madness. One day you will be parents too, and perhaps it will be easier to understand their lunacy, though not necessarily to forgive it.

It would also be helpful to be forewarned. And, with this in mind I have set my team to work on an A-Z of different types of parents. Because, remember, it isn't only your own parents you need to worry about. They can be handled, and even become quite house-trained (if you have the patience). No. It's *all* parents that you need to be wary of.

My team of "experts", for want of a better word, have sallied forth, and fifth, gathering data, which I then personally sifted, catalogued, and threw away. From it I made the following Parental Guide. I also made a paper aeroplane.

And what lengths they went to! Professor A. Doctor developed his own "Fly-On-The-Wall" technique. Or, more properly, "Fly-On-The-Shoe" technique, disguising himself as a fly, and positioning himself on a piece of dog dirt. Thus he was able to enter several homes on the soles of parents' shoes. In this way he obtained some extraordinarily frank footage.

Overall, my experts' research is an almost endless catalogue of in-depth interviewing, fearless exposure and (unfortunately for me) chequebook journalism. Prepare yourselves for a few surprises as we lift the lid off that (very wriggly) can of worms that is . . . THE A—Z OF PARENTS!

A is for
Ambitious Parent

The nature of the beast:
This particular type of parent appears to be fulfilling their own dreams, fantasies and ambitions via their child. Their own dreams of fame and fortune remaining unrealized, their offspring become the torch-bearer.

Habitat:
Mainly in the Home Counties and Thames Valley areas, although there are pockets of this particular breed "Up North". They are seen in great numbers at junior talent shows, dance schools, junior theatre workshops, etc. Although their ambition is not necessarily confined to theatrical matters, many of this type have realized that you don't have to be bright to succeed in show business. Gaz Top, Rusty Lee and Timmy Mallett are living proof of this.

Appearance:
The male of the species tends to wear a suede car-coat (and drive a suede car), with fake fur collar. This is seen as being in line with a "beauty without cruelty" attitude. After all, suede isn't animal skin, is it? I mean, there's no such animal as a suede, is there? Only a vegetable. The female wears an orange or purple (or both) fun-fur coat. This is partly for environmental reasons, and partly because it's cheaper than the real thing. These people are not rich, despite the name-dropping. Oh, they may have been once, but all their money has gone on dancing classes, voice lessons, and tap shoes for their child protégé.

Conversation:
The following was obtained with a microphone, cleverly hidden (but never recovered) about the person of Robert the Dachshund, who wormed his flea-bitten way into the

hearts and around the legs of a gathering of this particular breed of parent, at a wine and cheese party given by the Ivy Grunting Academy of Dance, Drama and TV Adverts. Ivy herself looked glorious, dressed as she was from head to foot in green tulle. Unfortunately, Robert mistook her for a tree, and got thrown out, but not before he obtained this recording:

"Well, she started at school when she was, oh, very young. She was in "The Dream" — although it turned out to be more of a nightmare in fact! Ha! Ha! Now, since Ivy has taken her under her wing, Sherry has really blossomed.

She's quite a chatterbox at home, although you'd never guess it, would you darling? (*Silence from Sherry.*) Anyway, Ivy pointed out that, these days, you've got to have a gimmick. It isn't enough just to be talented. Look at Bonny Langford — ooops! Listen to me name-dropping! — I mean, she not only sings but she shatters glass and frightens dogs at the same time! Well, Sherry's taken up juggling fish. Cod, actually. I don't know where she gets it from. Well, I do. We get it from Sainsbury's. Very good cod, they do there. Perfect for juggling. But I mean I don't know where she gets the talent from. I'm all fingers and thumbs when it comes to juggling cod. It's the eyes I think. I can't stand them staring at me. I suppose you could cut the heads off, but then you'd be juggling cod-pieces, which isn't the same thing at all, really. What? Her name? Sherry? . . . yes, it *is* an unusual name, isn't it? She's called Sherry after her grandmother, who drank too much of it."

Why this breed is dangerous:
Because very often the offspring want no part of the life that is being carved out for them. Some offspring counteract the effects of their parent's ambition by being so appallingly bad at everything that the parent eventually turns its attention to the younger, and often cuter, brother or sister. But be warned: this tactic can misfire. Total lack of talent can make you an overnight success (the examples of this are too numerous to mention!)

B is for
Boastful Parent

The nature of the beast:
Not to be confused with the Ambitious Parent. Being a Boastful Parent is a good deal cheaper, because they don't actually have to pay out for any training for the skills that they claim their child has.

Habitat:
All over the country. They tend to congregate anywhere that a group of similar parents might be found: at football matches (they're the ones in the stands. They wouldn't dare go on the terraces), in bars, working men's clubs, clubs generally, and at sports centres. Unlike the Ambitious Parent, it tends to be the male of the species who is the most vocal about their child's supposed talents.

Appearance:
Tracksuits, jogging suits, anything to hide the sagging body. However, these garments must have a designer name-tag on them, although they are rarely the real thing.

Conversation:
Sam "Fingers" Golightly obtained the following during a lunchtime session at the "Weary Jogger" Public House and Steak Eatery, newly built under the fly-over near Sam's maisonette. Sam believes that this will put thousands of pounds on to the value of his house. So far all it has done is put exhaust fumes all over his wife's washing. Sam, it must be admitted, does fall into this category himself, as will be shown in the transcript of the conversation:

Voice one: No, my lad's just got his "O" level results. Not bad, even if I do say so myself.

Voice two: What's he got?

Voice one: Five As and three Bs

Sam: Not bad.

Voice two: Huh! My lad got twelve As

Voice one: Ah, yes, but you have to remember that my boy had hearing difficulties until he was seven. So he's done very well.

Sam: Well, it was touch and go with our Sharon when she was born, but she's really shaped up.

Voice two: Listen: my lad was a bunch of bananas when he was born, but extensive surgery has made him the genius he is today.

Voice one: You told me he was a rhododendron bush.

Voice two: Yes. That as well. It stunned the whole of medical science. He's had books written about him.

Sam: Well, our Sharon's been on *London Plus*. When she won *Mastermind*.

Voice one: Huh! My lad could do that with his hands tied behind his back.

Voice two: Mine could do it with both hands tied behind his back, and one foot stuck up his nose.

Voice one: Mine could do it with his hands tied behind his back, *both* feet up his nose, and hanging upside down in a bucket of semolina.

Voice two: Mine could do it . . .

(*At this point the voices fade, as Sam slinks off out of the bar, unable to keep up.*)

Why this breed is dangerous:

I would have thought it was obvious! But one reason is that one day their children might meet each other.

C is for
Cautious Parent

The nature of the beast:
Extremely timid. A person to whom nothing more dangerous than a splinter in the finger has ever happened, but it just might! And that's the fear. Not for themselves, though. But for their child.

Habitat:
Health centres, school Open Days. But mostly to be found at home, watching their child travel to school, through a high-powered telescope, or pacing the floor until they return. Very occasionally they go to the park for exercise.

Appearance:
Bespectacled. Although the glasses may well contain plain glass (toughened, of course). This is to prevent a passing bicycle from flicking a small piece of killer-grit up into their eye. They also wear a sensible anorak, which they wear on every single (rare) trip out of doors, all year round. And wellies. In fact their house has probably been fitted with a wellie and anorak porch, through which it is impossible to pass unless you first put on (going out) or take off (coming in) your anorak and wellies. This parental type can be either sex. It's usually difficult to tell, as they dress identically. Their child would look the same, except that it is probably wrapped in cotton wool. That's what the bundle was in the picture, in case you thought that it was washing. Washing - that's another thing this breed does an awful lot of.

Conversation:
Very limited. It usually consists of short commands such as "Careful!" "Not so fast!" "Don't do that!" "Not on there!", etc. These are usually uttered in a voice that is strained. Not so much with panic, but with the desire to

sound unconcerned, relaxed and natural. It still comes out as a squeak.

Why this breed is dangerous:
The main reason is because they very rarely venture out of the house. And, as you know, the vast majority of accidents happen in the home!

D is for
Doting Parent

The nature of the beast:
Again, not to be confused with the Cautious Parent. The Doting Parent has no fears of anything untoward happening to their offspring, because their offspring can do nothing wrong, not even break a leg. Their child is simply perfect in every way. And this is quite different from the Boastful Parent, who just boasts, whether they actually believe it or not. This parent believes it. If you had the choice, this might well be the model to go for, although I think that it would get very tiresome very quickly. You would be forever looking for new and more outrageous ways of getting told off, and not succeeding.

Habitat:
Almost anywhere, although there are probably more of them in the more "monied" regions of the country. Doting can be a bit of a luxury which not every parent can afford, as it does take up a good deal of their time.

Appearance:
Again, there are no specific tell-tale signs, such as a big coat or a funny hat. The only way to tell a Doting Parent is to look in their eyes. There is a faraway look. If you've ever seen anyone in love, it looks a bit like that. Only worse, if that's possible. Piles can also give some people this look, so the system isn't infallible. Also, in the case of Doting Grandparents, the look can be caused by the battery in their pacemaker running down. So, if you're in any doubt, a very loud shout or a sharp kick may solve the problem. A loud shout will get you a clout from the Un-Doting Parent. A sharp kick is less reliable, however, as it will cause both a Doting, or an un-Doting Grandparent whose battery is running out, to fall over. So be careful.

Conversation:

Again, there is very little specific conversation. They tend to be too busy doting. They don't gather anywhere and swap stories with other Doting Parents, as they are not boasters. They just tend to greet everything their child does with the same doting smile. This can be as infuriating for visitors as it can be for the child in question. The child looks for more and more extreme ways of provoking a natural human reaction from their parent, and pretty soon this means attacking the visitors.

Should you ever find yourself cast in the role of visitor, don't make the (sometimes literally) fatal mistake of thinking, "I won't say anything. In a minute the parents are going to tell this child off." *Wrong*!

If you are the child in question don't make the (equally potentially fatal) mistake of thinking, "I can do what I like to this visitor. No one will harm me." This kind of thinking can lead to you suddenly discovering that the very nice man from next door, whose beard you are currently setting on fire, has a very short temper (and a long reach). And, as his hands tighten around your throat, what does your Doting Parent do? Come to your aid? Call the police? No. They start photographing it for the extremely large family album.

Why this breed is dangerous:

E is for
Embarrassing Parent

The nature of the beast:
Picture the situation. You have just started a new school. You have made some new friends. As a gesture of friendship, you invite these new friends to your home. Almost as the invitation leaves your mouth, you regret it. You suddenly remember that your parents will be there. Why should this matter? Your friends will understand. Everyone has parents. Not like yours, they don't, for yours are *embarrassing*. What is worse, you have no way of knowing how embarrassing they are going to be. On a scale of one to ten, it could be about three, something like pretending they really know about the music scene, and asking your mates if they've got "the latest Long Player by Adam and the Ants". Or it could be the Big Embarrassment, a ten. They are trying on their fancy dress costumes for the Round Table Dinner. So you arrive home and they are dressed as chickens. They then make matters worse by keeping the costumes on, and "entertaining" your friends by doing chicken impressions. Who needs it? You certainly don't! Parents should be seen and not heard. For preference, they should be *not* seen and not heard. In fact, the ideal situation would be that you never saw them, but they left messages, food parcels and money in a hollow tree in the garden, a bit like the KGB. But they don't.

Appearance:
That's the problem with the Embarrassing Parent. Unless they are actually wearing a chicken costume, they can look almost normal, and then it's very difficult to tell just how embarrassing they are going to get. Will it stop at showing your friends the baby photos, or will it go further? The video of you naked on the rug? Sitting on the potty? Or will Dad do his magic act? Paul Daniels he isn't!

74

Conversation:
All I can say is that you should just hope that they have been struck down by some mystery throat virus which renders them totally speechless. That is the only way you can be sure of what they might say. Otherwise, any subject under the sun might come up. The more intimate the better, as far as they are concerned. And if you think they are bad in front of your friends, wait until you take home your first boy/girl friend. That's when they really pull out the stops! I have no idea (and my researchers have also drawn a blank) why a parent should imagine that any of your friends should be interested in a potted history of your bowel movements. But they seem to think that this is a fit topic for discussion over the tea table:

> **Dad**: Pass the sausage rolls, will you, dear . . . that reminds me. I'll never forget the first perfect motion that young Jane here passed, will you, dear?

> **Mum**: I certainly won't. It really brought tears to her little eyes, didn't it? She went positively purple, do you remember, Jane dear? Jane? Jane! Sit up, dear! Why are you sliding under the table like that?

Why this breed is dangerous:
If you've never had a bodily function, never spoken, moved, passed wind . . . if, in fact, you are a cardboard cut-out, you have nothing to fear. Otherwise, there is no escaping the Embarrassing Parent! Sorry!

F is for
Fast-Food Parent

The nature of the beast:
They live life in the fast lane, or at least they like to think
they do. In fact, they're just very badly organized.
Consequently they feed you entirely on fast food. Do you
know, there are children going around who think all food
is round and covered in cardboard? Not that it is
necessarily bad for you. The average quarter-pounder
contains enough preservatives to make it last 126 years. So
just think how long you'll live with all that stuff inside you!
126 years! That's incredible. Why do they call it fast food,
if they are expecting it to hang around that long? Doesn't
make sense!

Habitat:
In fact, one of their habitats might well be "Habitat"
itself, because it does sell a sort of fast furniture. Not that
it's built to last 126 years, of course. (I mean, it might be,
but it doesn't — not in my experience, anyway!) But the
more obvious place to find this particular breed of parent
is in the queue at MacDonalds.

Of course, the really experienced Fast-Food Parent will
take all the family out (all 17 children) and place each child
in a different queue in a different shop, then dodge from
queue to queue. That way they get all their shopping done
in a seventeenth of the time. Brilliant, eh? Then it's off to
the burger bar for a slap-up meal. In some burger bars the
food is literally slapped up.

Appearance:
Fast food requires fast clothes — the ones that you don't
need to wash. Or, rather, the ones that you quickly
discover don't improve with washing. The Fast-Food
Mum would wear paper knickers, if they still make them.

Do they still make them? My researchers failed to turn up a single pair. But, then, none of my team are noted for their success with women.

Conversation:
One of the team managed to get this unique recording of a Fast-Food Mum ordering a meal for 17 children and two adults in a well-known burger bar.

> **Mum**: "Right . . . it's ten Quarter-Pounders, two Big Macs, three Chilli-Burgers, two Chicken-Burgers, two portions of Chicken Nuggets and 19 portions of chips . . . What? Who doesn't want chips? Oh! 18 chips, then. What? Make yer mind up! OK, OK! Three chicken Nuggets, only two Chilli-Burgers . . . what? Right . . . Oh! Hang on! Right! Does anyone want Chilli-Burger? No? Right! So that's . . . what? You don't want Pickles? Well, leave it! Don't cry! Right! Ten Quarter-Pounders, one no pickles, two Big Macs, three Chicken-Burgers, four Chicken Nuggets, 18 chips. Is that it? Who doesn't want Chilli? Have I got you one? Stop crying, unless you want a smack! Right! Is that it? (*To assistant*) That's it!
> **Assistant**: (*pleasantly*) Any drinks? (*Sound of a baby-buggy being thrown through a large plate-glass window*)

Why this breed is dangerous:
This breed is not dangerous, as long as you know exactly what you want to eat. Or you can duck.

G is for
Generous Parent

The nature of the beast:

This is a great type of parent to have, as long as you like watching people enjoying themselves. They have one driving force. And that is contained in the saying: "I want my kids to have everything I never had". And they really do mean everything. It's the sort of parent who has to hire a removal van to deliver the Easter eggs. We are talking Serious Generosity here. We all know the dad who gets a train set so that he can play with it himself. That's chicken feed to this parent. Their child is put down for every public and private school in existence. They own a horse at the age of two, a dolphin at five, shares in Telecom by the time they go to school, and an entire roomful of Masters of the Universe. That on top of the usual dog, cat, hamster, gerbil, tropical fishtank, guinea pig, python, Shetland pony and personal servant.

Habitat:

Unless they are a major villain, or have endless supplies of money, they probably live in a shoebox. Or, more probably, at the top of a block of shoeboxes, rented of course.

Appearance:
Clothes: well, yes. Perhaps. More likely they are dressed in trendy figure-hugging bin-liners.

Conversation:
The average conversation usually centres around the latest toy, gadget, etc. It may go like this:

Dad: Look at this, Simeon (*Simeon*!!). It's brilliant! It's Conan the Librarian! It's got moving limbs, realistic sneer, and a taped vocabulary of useful phrases, such as "Ugh!", "I've got you cornered", and "Oh, no! Those dog biscuits were poisoned!" Isn't that brilliant! You've nearly got the whole set of 56,987, haven't you? Well, we'll have to see what Father Christmas brings you, won't we? Hang on! What's this parcel here? Gosh! It's a complete university cap and gown and the colours for a Doctorate in Astrophysics. Well, you'll have to do well in your spelling test now, won't you?"

But Simeon can't hear. He has been entirely smothered by a mass of festive wrapping paper.

Why this breed is dangerous:
The biggest danger with this type of parent is the feeling that, one day, they may want a return on their investment!

H is for
Harassed Parent

The nature of the beast:
There are some parents who, on meeting them, make you feel amazed that they ever became parents at all. The simplest thing seems to send them into total chaos. Some of them, of course, go on to being Fast-Food Parents, but only after seeking medical help.

Habitat:
They live in a state of permanent panic, in almost any part of the country, although there may be less of them in large industrial areas. They are often called professional people. Professional people very often make very amateur parents. That's deep, isn't it? But true in many cases. They wear clothes with lots of pockets, which tend to be stuffed with all sorts of things that they imagine they may need: plasters, sweets, laxatives, etc. So therefore they are permanently on stand-by for every eventuality. They can't go on a day trip in anything smaller than a removal van.

Appearance:
Harassed. In a permanent untidy state, due to much rushing and panicking. But, unlike the Cautious Parent, they are not panicking about any imagined danger that might befall their child. They are panicking about

"getting it right". For they have read all the books. They have read Doctor Spock. But he might as well have been a Vulcan with pointy ears for all the good it's done them. From day one they got things wrong. Mum panicked about not being able to breastfeed. So did Dad. Then the doctor pointed out that Dad would not be called upon to breastfeed, and Dad relaxed. A little. Dad put the first nappy on the baby's head. I won't tell you where he put the bottle. And so it has gone on.

Conversation:
Should you happen to have one (or two) of this particular breed of parent, you will already know that even the simplest conversation can sound like an interrogation scene from *The Bill*.

You: Mum?
Mum: Er. Yes?
You: Have you seen my games kit?
Mum: Erm. Is that the white stuff?
You: Off-white. Yes.
Mum: Was I supposed to wash it?
You: Not really.
Mum: Oh. Good.
You: Have you seen it?
Mum: Yes.
You: Where?
Mum: Why?
You: I need it.
Mum: What for?
You: We've got games today.
Mum: Have you?
You: Yes. Where is it?
Mum: Your kit?
You: Yes.
Mum: D'you need it?

You: Yes!
Mum: What — now?
(*And so it goes on*)

Unfortunately she never keeps it up long enough for you to completely miss games. Just long enough for you to get into trouble for being late for school. And how can you explain that you were late because your mother was afraid to tell you where she'd put your games kit in case she was supposed to have put it somewhere else? Although a games kit does seem to have a life of its own, doesn't it? It's the one thing that always manages to be in the wrong place at the wrong time. In the bag when it should be in the wash, in the wash when it's supposed to be on your back. It's probably part of a plot by some alien life-force to destabilize the playing fields of England, and thus take over the world. (If it is part of some alien plot, it seems to be working as far as the England team are concerned, doesn't it?)

Perhaps if Spock had explained this in his baby book all those years ago (before he became an actor), your Mum wouldn't be so worried.

Why this breed is dangerous:
Well, unless you take charge of the situation and sort out the muddle yourself, you're in danger of walking around naked, and possibly even starving to death!

I is for
Inquisitive Parent

The nature of the beast:

If you're inclined towards having secrets, then this type of parent is one to be avoided. If yours are like this, I feel very sorry for you. They want to know everything that you're doing. Not usually for any deeply sinister reason. It's just that they're interested. It's idle curiosity. That's all. Although that doesn't explain all the surveillance equipment, the bugs in your telephone and the two-way mirror in the bathroom. You thought Big Brother was watching you, didn't you? Actually it's your parents. So, if you walk into your bedroom, see your Mum, say hello, and she jumps fourteen feet into the air, starts dusting with an invisible duster, and tells you that she's looking for a lost library book — in your underwear drawer, then you'll now know what's going on.

Habitat:

Almost anywhere, although they do tend to favour somewhere with a really good view, preferably high up so that there is little or no interference with radio signals from the homing device they've had secretly implanted in your lower wisdom tooth by a "bent" dentist. You thought he'd put you out for a long time, didn't you? Now you know why!

Appearance:

So that they can pry subtly into your every move, their senses have been highly developed for maximum sensitivity. That is to say, they've got big ears. Probably unnecessarily thick glasses too, and a large nose, for detecting cigarette smoke on your breath or clothes. Parents seem to forget totally that you don't have to smoke to smell of fags. Anyone who comes within a forty-mile radius of a lit cigarette immediately smells like an ashtray.

Conversation:

The average conversation with this type of parent is a bit like meeting the Spanish Inquisition:

> **Mum**: (*calling upstairs*) Where are you?
> **You**: In the loo.
> **Mum**: What are you doing?
> **You**: EH?!
> **Mum**: What are you doing?
> **You**: What do you think I'm doing?
> **Mum**: That's what I'm asking *you*!
> **You**: I'm on the toilet.
> **Mum**: Yes . . . ?
> **You**: Well, that's what I'm doing.
> **Mum**: What are you doing on the toilet?
> **You**: I'm boiling an egg.
> **Mum**: Don't be cheeky!

And she's not happy until she has every gory detail. I don't know why she bothers. She's probably got it all on tape somewhere, anyway. But this is the kind of parent who has to get it from the horse's mouth. The kind who always greets you in the morning with, "Have you had your bowels open?" And rest assured that when you're fifty, with a grown-up family of your own, your Mum will still be asking you the same question! And she'll always want to check your underwear before you go out of the house to make sure that it's clean (in case you get run over, apparently!).

Why this breed is dangerous:
Because you'll never have a life of your own. Some people think that this behaviour is possessiveness, or love. It isn't. It's nosiness, pure and simple.

J is for
Jolly Parent

The nature of the beast:

All sunshine and smiles. If you like life to be one endless round of chuckles and giggles, then this type is for you. Life with the Jolly Parent is a bit like living in a holiday camp. That is to say, the beds are too small and there's an outbreak of salmonella every five minutes. Only joking! That's this type of parent's catchphrase — *only joking*. And they usually are.

Everything is riotously funny. You break your leg: "Never mind. You've got another one!"

You fail all your exams: "Cheer up! You can always do them again." *Do them again*?!?! You didn't even want to do them the first time!

"Cheer up. It may never happen." That's another thing the Jolly Parent says. But don't they realize that it's the fact that it may never happen that's making you look so miserable in the first place! Whatever *it* might be!

Habitat:

Anywhere that you might find jolly people, such as in the back rows on coaches, leading the singing. Some Jolly Parents even try to get everyone singing on aeroplanes. On beaches they are the ones trying to force their kids into the sea in sub-zero temperatures. "If you're at the seaside you must go swimming" is the philosophy.

They're also the ones who turn the garden hose on you when you go into the garden to show them the (very expensive) new clothes you've bought. Clothes that cost you an arm and a leg. And you are proud that the years of skimping and saving and going without luxuries like chocolate eggs have been worthwhile. That you've finally found something to wear that makes you look the business, instead of all those things that your parents want you to wear: clothes that look just like school uniform in a different colour. But does your "playful" father ("call me Pop") think about this before he turns the hose on you, shrinking your clothes and giving you double pneumonia? Of course no! But, grin and bear it. It's only a bit of fun, after all. A bit of a laugh. What a card! He should be on telly!

Appearance:
Here the Jolly Parent rivals the the Embarrassing Parent. On holiday, they are the ones in the "Kiss Me Quick" hat, the "I'm With This Idiot" T-shirt. Oh, and sandals with socks! Now, that *is* funny, although it's not meant to be. This is the type of parent who dresses up as Father Christmas at Christmas, and an Easter Bunny at Easter. The type of Dad who dresses as a woman for charity (and fun!), and the type of Mum who enters the PTA Pancake Fun Run.

Conversation:

At great personal risk to herself, Eve-May Foskett (Mrs) took a part-time job as a daily help in a "Jolly" household. With a portable tape recorder concealed in the handle on her hoover, she was able to obtain the following recording. Unfortunately the hoover was turned on for much of the recording, and therefore some of the speech was impossible to hear. I have left these sections out:

(*Hysterical laughter*) Yes! That was funny, wasn't it? Cor! The look on her face! I nearly died! Nearly as funny as the time we put the jelly and ice-cream in the vicar's ★★★★★★★ ★★★ and it stuck on the ★★★★★★ of the table after it melted. You're a ★★★★★★★★ Mrs Foskett. Sorry there's such a mess, but we had a ★★★ ★★ ★ ★★last night. Actually it was Mandy's birthday. It was so ★★★★★. When she got up, we all pretended that we'd forgotten! Laugh! I'd thought I'd ★★★. It was a bit cruel, but, after all's said and done, she only cried for seven hours, and was almost cheerful by two in the morning. We played Hunt the Thimble, Hide the Custard, and then we ★★★★★★★ with some of those long balloons. My Alf challenged all the other dads to eating forty-two dog biscuits in less than a minute. He's the local ★★★★★★. Then we played Toss the Trifle, and had a whelk-eating contest. I expect that's what made Mrs Riley throw up. Kids? Oh, we didn't invite any kids. Kids are far too messy!

Later, when Mrs Foskett emptied the hoover-bag, she found some of the missing words. They were:

Trouser Leg, Bottom, Treasure, Bit Of A Do, Funny, Die, Champion, Played.

Though not necessarily in that order.

Why this breed is dangerous:

Dangerous is an understatement. This type of parent should carry a Government Health Warning!

K is for
Keen Parent

The nature of the beast:
"If a thing's worth doing, it's worth doing well". This could be the maxim of the Keen Parent, even if it does sound like a line from *Neighbours*. They take the business of being a parent extremely seriously (Keen Parents, I mean, not the cast of *Neighbours*). They read all the available books. In fact they probably wrote all the available books, not to mention being responsible for all the television programmes, fact-packs, videos, lecture-tours, and everything else that has been specially created to make the rest of the parents feel totally inadequate. It is probably Keen Parents who decide what is good for you and what isn't. They're the ones who keep changing their minds, too. You know the sort of thing: one day they say milk is good for you, next day they say it's too high in polyunsaturates. Well, whose fault is that? Who put the poly-thingies in there in the first place?

I'm convinced that *they* tell you that a thing is good for you if they've got a lot of it to get rid of. Think about it. They used to say that butter was bad for you. What happened? The EEC, or Common Market, ended up with a butter mountain. So now they say that butter is OK. In fact, every other advert on telly is for butter. They want us to eat it until it comes out of our ears. Let's hope they never get a baked bean mountain!

Habitat:
School Open Evenings. Keen Parents are the ones who ask the really difficult questions. That's a waste of time, isn't it? I mean, if teachers were clever enough to answer really difficult questions, they wouldn't be teachers, would they? They'd get proper jobs. Keen Parents are also the ones who hang about afterwards to talk to the teacher:

DO YOU THINK JOHN IS HYPER INTERACTIVE OR JUST INVOLVEMENT MOTIVATIONAL?

Parent: How is our son, James, doing in English?
Teacher: Very well. Very well indeed. He's a credit to you. His progress has been remarkable. Quite remarkable. Several of the staff have remarked on his progress. You should be very proud of him . . . Which one *is* James, exactly?

They also spend hours going through your work. Trying to work out which subject is which. Trying to work out what you've written ("With this handwriting, the lad could be a doctor!"). It isn't easy being a Keen Parent, so they tell us.

They are also the ones at Sports Day, who spend hours holding the rope, or manning the stopwatch (sorry — person-ing the stopwatch), or tying the legs of the three-legged race contestants together. Or untying the legs of the Deputy Head, who isn't in the three-legged race but has been set up by some of the older boys.

Keen Parents are also the ones who offer to help "backstage" at the School Nativity Play. They're the ones who get the job of hanging on to the rope that causes the Angel Gabriel to fly. You can see them, pulling, cursing, (though never blaspheming), and muttering under their breath: "Show me the bit in the Bible that says the angel Gabriel was fifteen stone!" But they soldier on, for they are keen.

Appearance:
They need to be prepared for every eventuality. Therefore they have the look of someone who could spring into action at a moment's notice. Rather like a sprinter on the block. Or, as Shakespeare put it, "Like a greyhound in the slips". I find that strange. I wouldn't have thought that Shakespeare would have known anything about greyhound racing. If I were a Keen Parent, I would research that and find out! The keen parent is ever-ready for that all-important phone call from the PTA Bring-and-Buy White Elephant Stall Replenishment Sub-Committee Steering Group.

Conversation:
Well, to be honest, they are so busy working at being the ideal parent to their offspring, that they don't really have much time left to talk.

Why this breed is dangerous:
I would have thought this was obvious. You see, the Keen Parent has lots of energy for their role in life, and all this energy is directed at their child. Now, you don't need to be a Professor of Astrophysics to work out that that much energy, pointed in one direction, could have devastating effects.

L is for
Loving or Lousy Parent

The nature of the beast:
The Lousy or Loving Parent is often one and the same thing. Because they love you so much, they find it hard to be a good parent.

Habitat:
They live in a house full of love, but very little else. I have nothing against love. Love is wonderful. But I also like fish fingers, burgers, chips. You can't eat love, can you?

Appearance:
Well — loving, really.

Conversation:
Very little conversation. Oh, obviously there is the occasional bit about how much they love you. But they have great difficulty with ordinary conversations. A typical conversation will go along the lines of:

You: Mum?
Mum: Yes, love?
You: Have you seen my football kit?
Mum: No, love. (*She kisses you*)
You: Oh.

What else can you say? After all, you know she loves you. You know she'd walk to the ends of the earth for you. But you don't want her to walk to the ends of the earth for you. Just as far as the shops would do.

Why this breed is dangerous:
With this parent, you'll never want for love. But you *could* starve to death.

M is for
Modern or Media Parent

The nature of the beast:

Self-expression. This is one of the things that the Modern Parent believes in. Washable wallpaper was created specifically for this parent. Your little brother scribbles all over the wall: he is expressing himself. You scribble all over the wall: you get a thick ear! Except, you don't. For corporal punishment is something this parent does *not* believe in. However, by the time they've finished explaining how disappointed in you they are, your ear is hurting just as much. So they might as well have bashed it in the first place! The children of this particular breed of parent are allowed to call them by their first name.

You: Dad?
Dad: Oh, for heavens sake! Call me Jolyon!
You: Call you *what*?

You are also privileged to see them with no clothes on. In fact, they almost insist on it: "No mysteries around here!" But, having seen your Dad with nothing on, you realize that the biggest mystery is what on earth does your Mum see in him?

Parents should be very careful about exposing their naked flesh to their children. It could frighten them for life! It was Shakespeare, that famous poet, playwright and greyhound fancier, who said: "Let her paint an inch thick, to this favour must she come." (He also said: "There's something rotten in the state of Denmark." I think he was refering to the EEC butter mountain.)

Of course, many Modern Parents would know a good deal about Shakespeare. For many of them are Media Folk. More of that later.

Habitat:
The home of the average Modern/Media Parent tends to be either very spartan — the sort of house where it's almost impossible to find a chair — or very cluttered — the sort of house where it's equally impossible to find a chair. You will also find this breed in art galleries, where their smaller children add bits to famous paintings, or theatres, where their smaller children add hours to the play's running time by insisting on getting up on the stage. That's fine at a matinée performance of *Jack and The Beanstalk*, but it goes down less well at the Royal Opera House. (Although, of course, it's always possible that most of the audience will think it's part of the show, since very few of them understand opera, anyway.)

Appearance:
They dress as the mood takes them, and encourage their children to do likewise. I will give you an example. I once met a famous playwright. I won't mention his name because (A) it would embarrass him, and (B) you will probably never have heard of him. However, he brought his family to watch a performance of one of his plays that I was in. After the show, the cast lined up to be presented to them. He had a large family, all of whom appeared to be wearing curtains. They were in fact wearing waistcoats made out of curtains. One of them also wore a fireman's helmet (his wife was positively underdressed in a radiation suit). Waistcoats made out of curtains! It might look OK in *The Sound of Music* but it looked very strange in the Tidsbury Art Centre!

Conversation:
In my capacity as "Friend of the Stars" (I've met Lionel Blair), I often have to rub shoulders with (shorter) Media Folk. It was therefore quite easy for me to gather the following piece of conversation myself, at a recent

riverside party to launch a new range of male cosmetics endorsed by the Welsh International Rugby team. The recording would have been longer, but a group of estate agents gate-crashed the party and threw me in the river, which had a bad effect on my batteries (the batteries in the recorder were fine). Why did the estate agents pick on me? Perhaps it had something to do with the fact that I was the only one who didn't own seven houses:

"The christening was a dream. I mean, we don't, you know, *believe*, but I think you owe it to *them*, don't you?"
"Absolutely."
"I think so."

"What did you call her?"

"Tamsin."

"That's unusual. Is it Biblical?"

"No. Actually it's a rather attractive boat builder's putty that we saw featured on *Howard's Way*. Anyway, the captain performed the ceremony, which was a little bit hairy. He rather overdid the champagne."

"What? D'you mean he was squiffy?"

"No. I mean when he cracked the bottle over poor Tamsin's head. That's how they name things in the navy, you know."

Why this breed is dangerous:
The most frightening thing about a Modern/Media Parent is the fact that you could grow up to be just like them. What a thought!

N is for
Nagging Parent

The nature of the beast:
Earlier in the book, I mentioned that parents ask questions which they already know the answers to. Do you remember that? You can check, if you like. I don't mind waiting (I assume that it's a bit of the book that escaped Robert the Dachshund's unique form of editing). Found it? Good. Well, the Nagging Parent is the past master of this art. Not only the past master, but the present and the future master as well. And mistress, in the case of the Nagging Mum. They seem to spend their entire life questioning your actions, telling you that you shouldn't be doing what you're doing, even if it's the exact opposite of the last thing that you were doing which they told you that you shouldn't be doing. Confused? That's hardly surprising. Because *surprise* is the Nagging Parent's secret weapon.

Habitat:
In bushes, behind doors, under beds. In fact, anywhere that provides a bit of cover. Just when you thought it was safe to sit on the loo . . . the Nagging Parent strikes: "Why are you using so much lavatory paper?" Your life is not your own. You can't go anywhere or do anything without getting nagged.

And don't imagine you are safe when your parents are not with you. Because you're not! The thing about Nagging Parents is that they are quite happy to nag *anybody*. It doesn't have to be one of their *own* children. What makes it worse is the fact that this particular breed is very common. And what compounds the problem is the fact that the Nagging Parent, or, to give them their Latin name, *Naggus Tu Deathus*, is a distant cousin of that other difficult type, the Inquisitive Parent. You could be doing something fairly harmless — minor surgery on next door's Manx cat (at least, it's a Manx cat *now*, anyway), and totally unbeknown to you, the local snoop has got you recorded for posterity on their Inquisitive Parent's Surveillance Kit (available from all good health centres). Next thing you know, the Nagging Parent is giving you an earful of Relentless Verbal Porridge.

Appearance:
Ah! Here is where the Nagging Parent can be very devious. They look perfectly normal. Well, as normal as any parent ever looks. And, like a chameleon, they have the power to blend with their surroundings. That door could be a parent. That wardrobe could be one. That tallboy definitely is one (but at least he's come out of the closet!).

Out of doors, they don't exactly wear army camouflage gear, but they manage to blend in with the background, as they sneak from bush to bush ready to stop you doing whatever it is you're doing, however harmless. Oh, yes! These are devious animals!

Conversation:
This seems to consist mainly of phrases that begin: "Don't" or "Stop" as in:

"(Don't) do that!" or
"(Stop) that!"

"That" is their universal word to cover absolutely anything that you may, or may not, be up to. For, be assured, you don't actually have to be doing the thing you're accused of in order to get nagged.

Why this breed is dangerous:
A Doctor writes: Nagging can be extremely bad for anyone of a nervous disposition, or anyone not of a nervous disposition. In fact, anyone. Avoid it like the plague!

A Nother Doctor writes: The plague is also bad for you.

PESTER
BLAH
NAG BADGER
BADGER
NAG
BLAB
BLAB
NAG NAG
BLAH
nag
BLAB BLAB BLAB
NAG NAG
BLAH
NAG
BLAH
BLAH
BLAB
BADGER
BADGER
NAG
BLAH
NAG
BLAB
BLAH
NEEDLE
BLAB
GABABAB
GABAB
NAG
PESTER
NAG
BLAH
BLAH
GAB GAB
NAG
BLAH
PESTER
BLAH
nag-nag
BLAH
PECK
BLAB
HARASS
HARASS
NAG
GAB
GAB
NABBLE
BLAH
NAG
PECK
BLAH
NAG-NAG
BLAH
NAG
GAB NEEDLE
HARASS
BLAB
HARASS
NAG
HARASS
BITCH
BITCH
BITCH
Blah
Blah
Blah
BLAH
nag
NAG
Blah Blah
Blah
HENPECK
HENPECK
nag nag
BLAB
BLAB
GAB
GAB
NAG
BLAH
BADGER
BADGER
NAG NAG
BLAH
badger
badger
BLAH
nag nag
BLAH
NAG
nag nag
BLAB BLAB
NAG
NAG NAG
NAG NAG
BLAB NAG
HARASS
HARASS
HARASS
pester
pester
BLAH
BLAH
NAG
BLAH
BLAH
NAG
BLAB
BLAB
BLAB
BLAB
PESTER
PESTER
blag
blag
NAG
NAG
BLAB
BLAH Nag
nag nag
NAG-NAG
nag
nag BLAH
NAG
NAG NAG
NAG
NEEDLE
NEEDLE
BLAH
NAG-BLAH
BLAH
Blah
HARASS
HARASS
nag
NAG
NAG
badger
badger
BLAH

O is for
Obvious Parent

The nature of the beast:
There are, of course (obviously!), times when having this type of parent is a godsend. For instance, when you are six months old, and you are wondering who your mother is (or even wondering *what* your mother is), it can help to have this type of parent - the parent who is undeniably *yours*. But, naturally, as you get older, you want to be considered as an individual, even a young adult. But with this type of parent, it is impossible! For you are theirs, they are yours, and the world must be constantly aware of this fact.

Habitat:
Anywhere where a decent crowd could gather and point - school Open Evenings, Speech Days, the School Play, the Annual Burning of the School Caretaker Ceremony. That sort of thing. If there are plenty of your friends around, so much the better. But, don't confuse this type with the Embarrassing Parent. The Obvious Parent does not wish to embarrass you. Although the end result is often very similar. No. All they want to do is assert, publicly, that *they are your parents*. And, strangely, the more you try to get them to disown you by behaving outrageously, the harder they cling to the parental position.

Appearance:
This should be a dead give-away. The average Obvious Parent goes out of their way to look as much like their offspring as possible. Or rather, they make their offspring look like them. If it was the other way round then perhaps (only perhaps, mind you) it might be almost bearable. At least you wouldn't be the one looking a wally! But it isn't. The Obvious Parent invented cloning long before the scientists discovered it was possible.

Again, when you are young, it's a fun thing to dress up in your mum's clothes (it's less acceptable, by the way, when a man reaches about 35). But to be forced out of doors looking just like your parents, simply because they want people to know who you "belong to", is very hard to take. These parents are the sort who, when they were going out together, before they were married (you'll notice that, after marriage, parents rarely go out *at all* - certainly not together), these people used to wear those awful matching Aran sweaters with green reindeers on them. (Actually, have you seen how expensive those things are? No wonder it was years before your parents could afford their own house. They spent their life savings on a couple of sweaters!)

Conversation:
Tends to be limited to loud calls, in crowded shops, of:
    "Don't talk to me like that! I'm your Mother!" or
    "Ask your Father." Or, much worse,
    "Aren't you going to give your Mother a kiss, then?"

This last one is usually saved for well-attended school events.

Why this breed is dangerous:
A Doctor writes: There is a feeling in the medical world that it is not, in fact, possible to die of embarrassment. Personally I wouldn't chance it!

P is for
Perfect Parent

No information is available on this type of parent.

Q is for
Quiet Parent

The nature of the beast:
You would have thought, on the face of it, that this particular breed of parent would be ideal, wouldn't you? I mean, you're hardly aware of their existence, and they don't hassle you at all. In fact, you would almost believe that they didn't exist. You would be wrong!

Habitat:
Behind newspapers, deep in armchairs, in front of the telly, out at bingo, down the pub. More intelligent branches of this particular life-form can be found buried in books.

Appearance:
This is a difficult one. One of my team, Elderado
Dingbatti, conducted a survey among known possessors of
Quiet Parents. This was done in the form of a
questionnaire. Several thousand questionnaires, compiled
by Dingbatti himself, were sent out. Very few replies were
received, mainly because most of the children taking part
did not understand the questions. Elderado has a highly
developed talent for being completely incomprehensible
to the average person. However, from the answers we did
receive, a definite pattern emerged:

> Could you positively identify your parent in a police
> line-up?
> Yes . . .   0%
> No . . . 100%

However, from other answers received, it became
obvious that most of the children taking part had caught
glimpses, albeit fleeting ones, of their parents over the tops
of newspapers, going through doors (back view) etc. A few
even recalled seeing a hand as a meal was placed in front of
them, or an elbow as the table was cleared again, two arms
as a Father stretched in an armchair. One person actually
caught a glimpse of a buttock as their father stepped out of
the bath, but such sightings of this particular beast are
previously totally unheard of. (In fact, J Sedgewick of
Cockfosters, I have passed on the details of your Buttock
Sighting, if I may call it that, to the Guinness Book of
Records, and no doubt they will be in touch.

Conversation:
Again there is very little to go on. The art of conversation
as we know it seems to be quite foreign to this breed.
Indeed, in the case of Shirley Crump of Didcot, conversation is *completely* foreign, as her parents are both Italian.

The emerging pattern seems to suggest that most communication between the Quiet Parent and their offspring is done by note. We have recorded many instances of children coming home to find a note propped against the teapot, reading:

"Dinner in fridge".

This, roughly translated, means:

"There's a freezer full of frozen food, nearly all of which is on the listeria blacklist, which just needs defrosting, cooking and, if possible, eating".

There can be other, unwritten implications suggested by the note. For example:

"I will not be back for a very long time, so could you also feed the Rottweiler, the rubber plant, the baby, the goldfish, and the thing slumped in the chair which answers to the name of Dad".

Possibly *answers* is an exaggeration. The Quiet Dad speaks *fluent grunting*, a language that has never really achieved universal acceptance, except in the European Parliament, where they use it to discuss butter mountains.

Why this breed is dangerous:
So little is known about this type of parent, that it would be wrong to state categorically that this breed is dangerous. It may be entirely harmless. However, someone once said something about "the calm before the storm". You may find yourself lulled into a false sense of security and then overstep the mark, in some minor way. You may then find that the Quiet Parent is actually a Nagging Parent in disguise. The Nagger is *that devious*. So, beware!

R is for
Reluctant Parent

The nature of the beast:
There are those parents, believe it or not, who become parents almost by accident. It is not part of their great design, if indeed they had a great design in the first place. They are Reluctant Parents. Anne Expert found such a man. She sends us this profile:

Habitat:
Nestling in the heart of Yorkshire, deep in the Dales, amid the winding, windswept streets, just behind the gas works, we find a neat cluster of allotments. It is here that we find Arthur. He visits this, his private world, on an almost daily basis, where he sits among the cabbages and peas, tugging on a generous pipeful of Old Ogmore's Ready Cut Nut Shag, watching the rest of the world pass by, as it has for more than fifty years. Arthur recently made the birth columns of the *Amateur Gardener* and *Suet Pudding Farmer's Weekly*, when he became a father, totally unexpectedly. In fact the shock was so great that he very nearly made the births and deaths columns in the same issue. Apart from Arthur's age, what makes this event unique is that it seems to support the Stork theory, which has for many years been totally discounted by medical men and women the world over.

Appearance:
Arthur is an unprepossessing person, from his ex-army boots to the curls of smoke issuing from the nasal hairs, which have once again been ignited by a rogue spark from his trusty Briar pipe. The years have not been kind to him, and each disappointment is etched in the grime of the crumpled cow-pat he wears as a face. He has never been mistaken for Robert Redford. He may once have been mistaken for the back of a bus, when four youths jumped on him as he went up the High Street. That was their defence later in court, anyway.

Conversation:
Having convinced Arthur that the experience would not affect his dart throwing, which would remain bad, he agreed to talk into my Media Person-al Tape recorder. This is the basis of what he said. I have, naturally, edited out any extraneous noises, of the sort that you are bound to get from a person who lives almost entirely on organically grown fresh vegetables. Over to Arthur:

"Is it on? Well, I never really wanted to be a parent. I don't think me and the wife have ever actually talked about it, but I suppose if pressed I'd have to admit that I'm happy as I am. But, well . . . (pardon me) . . . it just happened. I was out in my allotment, attending to my gooseberry bushes. I've got some lovely big fruits, but, of late, sad to say, they've been plagued with a nasty dose of Murphy's Blight. Anyroadup, I was just rubbing linseed oil on the affected parts, as you do, and I noticed the little chap sitting there, bold as brass, and twice as naked. Nubbut a little fella he were, no bigger than . . . well, no bigger than a baby. Well, he looked so helpless that I thought I'd better tek 'im indoors. Well, my Missus, she takes one look at him and says, 'Just our luck!'.

Well, I thought, Oh, no! She hasn't been entering them competitions again, has she? You know the sort of thing: send five packet tops, answer a simple question, and you win a Ford Capri, or a baby. Well, we asks up and down the road, but nobody seemed to think it was theirs, or nobody seemed to want it anyway. Then the wife says: 'Why don't we keep it?'

'You great wassock!' I said. I always call her that when I'm mithered with her. That were her name, you see, before we were wed: Gertrude Wassock. Of course, she's a Bumplaster now. Cus that's my name. Arthur Bumplaster. She decided to take my name, after we was wed, so's not to confuse the postman.

Anyway, after a bit of a chat, and a bit of a fight, we decided to keep the baby (she has a mighty left hook, does the wife). So, we kept it, and — because the Wife's quite romantic for a Welter-Weight Boxing Champion — we named it after the place we found it. We called him Betty Street Municipal Allotments Limited plc, or Jonathan for short."

Why this breed is dangerous:
A Doctor writes: Dangerous is probably too strong a word. But certainly, if you could avoid being born under a gooseberry bush, and brought up by complete strangers, I think you'll find life a bit easier to cope with.

S is for
Superstitious Parent

The nature of the beast:
The Superstitious Parent believes that everything has a purpose. I'm not referring to religion. God's Masterplan is something completely different. I mean, we all know that if God had wanted you to be bored, He wouldn't have invented Lego. No. The Superstitious Parent is the type who has your astrological chart drawn up at the moment of your birth. (As if the delivery room wasn't full enough with all those doctors, nurses, storks, relatives taking photographs, and camera crews from Channel Four making documentaries. There's barely room for an astrologer as well, especially if he's the size of Russell Grant. Then there's his crystal balls (for gazing into), star charts, astrological calendar, slide rule, powerful telescope, and a copy of the star page of the *Sun* . . .)

Having a Superstitious Parent is all very well. I suppose it keeps your parents' minds off continually checking your feeding (and other!) habits. But, as far as your parent is concerned, all this stuff determines your character. It can't be true, can it? All Pisces people can't be the same, can they? If that were so, it would mean that all Geminis would be twins, all Cancerians would walk sideways, all Leos would chase zebras and all Aquarians would wet the bed.

Habitat:
This type of parent is often found in the astrology section of public libraries. Also in paper shops. They're the ones who don't buy anything. They just go through all the newspapers, reading and comparing the star columns. They are also found sneaking around the nursery. Some of this breed have actually learned to read nappies! It's true!

111

Awful, isn't it? I don't think I really want to poke about with this topic too much. They also study the actions of their offspring to determine their future. If you scribble on the wall, you're going to become a great artist. If you talk a lot, you're going to be a top politician. If you have permanent wind, you're going to invent an Alternative Organic Fuel. Knowing what you are actually going to be when you grow up can obviously have its advantages. It prevents all those hours of deliberation about whether to be a fireman or a famous popstar (why not both?). If only any of the superstitious nonsense was accurate.

Appearance:
From nowhere, more often than not. Just when you thought you had a few quiet moments to yourself to adjust the contents of your left nostril, the Superstitious Parent swoops, grabs their prize, and starts flicking through their copy of *Halliwell's Encyclopedic Guide to the Reading of Gilberts*. Actually, you can be fairly certain of what the future holds if you are picking your nose: someone will probably tell you to stop it. You don't need *Halliwell's Encyclopedia* to tell you that.

Conversation:
It is hard to have a straightforward conversation with the Superstitious Parent, because they want to know the underlying significance of everything you say:

   You: Morning, Dad.
   Dad: Why did you say that?
The worst thing is that you then start wondering yourself. Why did I say that?
   You: I said it because it is and you are.
Forget it. You are on a hiding to nothing.

Why this breed is dangerous:
A Doctor writes: It is a known medical fact that too much star-gazing can be fatal, particularly if you do it while walking along the street in heavy traffic.

T is for
Tyrannical Parent

The nature of the beast/Habitat/Appearance/Conversation:
All these aspects of the Tyrannical Parent can probably be
best described by this sketch:

You see, the Tyrannical Parent is actually a little person, trying to be a big person. Alternatively, they are a big person, with a nice little person struggling to get out. Somewhere along the line, they decided that, in order to command respect, they would have to shout.

Some teachers are like this. They would probably make very good Tyrannical Parents. I don't know whether you know this, but: TEACHERS CAN BE PARENTS, TOO!

They can! Terrible, isn't it? There's not a lot of evidence to suggest that the teacher/Tyrannical Parent gives their child lines if they're naughty. And there wouldn't be a lot of point keeping the child in and not allowing them home, would there? Because they are already at home! It must be tough being a parent *and* a teacher!

Why this breed is dangerous:
Knowing that the Tyrannical Parent isn't really a tyrant isn't a lot of help, I'm afraid. The tyrant needs to realize that they're not really a tyrant.

U is for
Umpire Parent

The nature of the beast:
Those of you who have brothers and/or sisters will know the value of a parent who can arbitrate in the event of a fight (ie, every other day). Such a beast is rare. But they do exist, in the form of the Umpire Parent.

Habitat:
Generally found in the home, or anywhere where there is sibling rivalry (ie, everywhere).

Appearance:
This particular parent may have the wisdom of Solomon, but they don't look like him. Actually, the wisdom of Solomon is always something that has confused me. Two ladies come before Solomon. They both claim to be the mother of the same baby. What does Solomon, in his infinite wisdom, suggest? Only that they chop the baby in half and have a bit each. Bit silly, I'd have said. Supposing the ladies had both said: "Cor! Brilliant! Great idea! Which bit do you want, Maureen?" What would he have done then, eh? I mean, he couldn't really turn round and say: "Sorry, girls! Only joking!", could he? After all, he was the Wise One, wasn't he? He'd look a bit stupid, wouldn't he? I reckon he was chancing his arm, not to mention the baby's arms, legs, and all points north and south. Doesn't sound too bright to me!

However, the quarrels that the Umpire Parent has to solve rarely involve anything so complicated as the problems of Solomon.

Conversation:
In these enlightened times, no argument can be solved with Dad saying: "Shut up you two, or I'll bang your heads together". These days everything has to go to

arbitration, very often involving both parents taking different sides.

The Umpire Parent has to weigh both sides of the argument carefully, taking all aspects into consideration, and then pass judgement. As in the case of Uptree versus Uptree:

The Defendant, Kevin Uptree, was accused on the 3rd of January 1989 of breaking the drinking bowl in the hamster cage of the Plaintiff, Jo-Anne Uptree. Appearing for the Defence, Shirley Uptree (Mum). Appearing for the Plaintiff, Daphne Uptree (Granny). Justice Uptree (Dad) presided. Arnold Uptree (Grandad) sat in a chair and snored. Clerk of the court (the dog), barked and generally kept order:

Gran: M'Lud, the defendant, one Kevin Uptree, stands accused of the crime of breaking the drinking bowl of one Pam, a hamster of this parish, the property of the Plaintiff, one Jo-Anne Uptree. It is our submission that the breaking was an act of deliberate agression against the person of my client.

Kevin: (*from the dock, well, the sofa really*) It was an accident!

Dog: Woof! (*Silence in court*)

Dad: What says the defence?

Mum: M'Lud. It is the defence's case that this action was taken in retaliation for names that the Plaintiff called my client.

Jo-Anne: Didn't!

Dog: Woof!

Mum: This name-calling was reported to my client by one Trevor Fishwick, who unfortunately cannot be here today.

Gran: Objection. That is hearsay evidence and is inadmissible.

Dad: Objection over-ruled.

Kevin: That's not fair!

Dog: Woof! (*bites Kevin*)

Kevin: Ouch!

Dad: The prisoner must be quiet. He will get his chance to defend his actions later. (*To dog*) Clerk of the court, stop biting the prisoner and get back in your basket.

Microwave oven: Beep! Beep! Beep!

Dad: Ah! Lunch is ready! Court will adjourn for one hour, and reconvene after the lunchtime edition of *Neighbours*.

Grandad: Snore.

Well, after the recess (lunch and *Neighbours*), the court reconvened to hear the history of the case. Claim and counterclaim were made. Events dating back many years were taken into consideration: the Plaintiff's locking of the Defendant in the lavatory on a trip to Aunty Vera's in Morecambe in 1984. The pulling of the Plaintiff's pigtails by the Defendant and several (un-named) accomplices. Eventually reports were called for, exhibits were examined: the broken drinking bowl, the headless "My Little Pony" from a previous argument, not to mention the seemingly endless catalogue of name-calling, face-pulling and arm-pinching. In all, 476 previous convictions were taken into consideration.

Eventually, Justice Uptree retired (to the Ferret's Rest Public House) to consider his verdict. In his summing-up he made much of the usual good conduct of both the Defendant and the Plaintiff. He said that the flare-ups between both parties were isolated incidents, and not proof of a growing trend. He bound both parties over to keep the peace (ie, shut up), and threatened that, if they did not follow his instructions, he would bang their heads together.

Why this breed is dangerous:
This breed is only really dangerous if you lose the argument!

V is for
Vague Parent

The nature of the beast:
It isn't always easy being a parent, as the Harassed Parent knows only too well. A distant cousin of the harassed breed is the Vague Parent. The Vague Parent has developed absent-mindedness into an artform. Maybe it's just an inability to cope, as with the Harassed Parent. More likely it's just an inability.

Habitat:
The Vague Parent is often to be found wandering aimlessly about in supermarkets, wondering what they came in for, and whether or not they had any children with them when they *did* come in.

Appearance:
Vacant, really. You always get the impression with the Vague Parent that they are somewhere else. And, as far as they know, they may well be! They don't really seem to know where they are. Or *who* they are for that matter.

Conversation:
A conversation with a Vague Parent is rather like talking to a total stranger. They are given to using phrases like: "That's nice, dear", or: "That's interesting". It doesn't really seem to matter what you've said!

You: Dad, I've just set fire to the garden shed.
Dad: That's nice, dear.

I suppose it's better than the Quiet Parent, who would just grunt. The Vague Parent doesn't even have the excuse that they are reading, watching telly, putting together an MFI self-assembly Sauna 'n Barbeque. No. You have their *undivided attention*. But you might just as well have their *divided attention*, or their *neatly cut into 'soldiers' attention*,

or even their *screwed up in a little ball* attention. None of it will make any difference! Because they don't really know who you are! And it doesn't stop at parents. Very often the Vague Parents give birth to Vague Children. Have you ever been to a fête or a Sports Day, and heard a tannoy announcement:

> "Would anyone who has lost a little boy please come to the refreshment tent next to the chemical toilets."

Why don't they say:

> "Would the parents of five-and-a-half-year-old Stephen Joystick from Hartlepool please come and collect him from the refreshment tent."?

They don't give all those details out because they don't know them! A little lost boy arrives, crying:

Boy: I've lost my Mummy.
Man: What's her name, sonny?
Boy: She's called Mummy.
Man: Well, what's your name?
Boy: Er . . .
Man: Well, what does your Mummy call you?
Boy: Little horror.
Man: Well, what does your Mummy look like?
Boy: She's got a dress on.
Man: Oh. Right. (*Into tannoy*) Would a woman in a dress please come and collect a little boy from the refreshment tent.

Pandemonium breaks out as women in dresses flock to the refreshment tent, thinking that they've won the star prize ("And here's me thinking I was just going home with a goldfish!"). Unfortunately for the lost boy, his Vague Mother doesn't realize that he's lost, doesn't want the star prize, and so doesn't go to the tent. Well, I say unfortunately for him, but he might do quite well out of the deal. He might get a much better breed of Mum.

Why this breed is dangerous:
On the one hand, they may forget to feed and clothe you. On the other hand, they may well forget that they've already given you your pocket money, so having a Vague Parent can be worked to your advantage!

W is for
Weekend or Working Parent

The nature of the beast:
In this day and age, it is far more common for parents to work (as long as you plug them in!). There has always been a breed of parent, however, who has refused to give up their career in order to raise a family. Why should they? But what this actually means is that all those little things that families do together — eat, play, fight — have to be crammed into the weekend. This can be especially true of Media Parents. It is also a fact that this particular parent is not satisfied with treating their offspring to a bit of fishing once a month, the occasional trip to an ice rink, the pictures once a year. Oh, no! They must expose their child to every form of activity going, even if it kills them (a trip to a rifle range can usually be guaranteed to do this). And so, it's early to bed on Friday night, because *the weekend starts here*!

Habitat:
Ice rinks, discos, cinemas, riding schools, drama clubs, music schools, dance schools, then off for a burger, if they can cram it in. Actually, cramming it in is usually the best way to eat a burger. Anything to avoid tasting it!

Appearance:
Well, naturally, the Weekend Parent would be dressed for the part!

Conversation:
I'm not sure there would be any time left to talk! But the average conversation would probably go something like:

> **You**: Look at me, Mummy!
> **Mum**: Yes, dear! But don't forget you're going scuba diving in three minutes!

Because we are talking *tight scheduling*!

Why this breed is dangerous:
A Doctor writes: Exercise in moderation is fine. Exercise in other places is fine too. It's the rushing about from place to place that'll probably finish you off!

X is for
Xylographic Parent

The nature of the beast:
Yes. All right. I can hear you thinking (do you always think aloud, by the way?): "He's finally flipped! Or run out of ideas! (which is more likely). "What's a *xylograph*?" I hear you cry.

Well, there's no need to cry. I'll tell you: a xylograph is a woodcut. So, if your parent was xylographic, they would be made of wood.

"That's silly! A parent can't be made of wood!" you shout. I didn't say they could. It might be nice though. There have actually been examples: Edward Woodward. Even the name is a giveaway. (And, if you've seen him in *The Equalizer*, you'll be convinced that he's made of wood!) Then there's the Wooden Tops — a perfect family unit, complete with 2.5 children and a dog. All made of wood. OK, so none of them wear shirts or blouses, but maybe there's a touch of the Modern Parent in there too. Then there's Annie Oakley, Leslie Ash, the whole of *Nightmare on Elm Street*, Stephanie Beecham, Harry Lime, Holly Johnson, and — of course — Ewe! Yes! All right! I am scraping the barrel! (Barrels are made of wood, too!)

Y is for
Youthful Parent

The nature of the beast:
There is no sight that tugs at the heart-strings more than that of a proud dad kicking a ball for his young don. And, incidentally, there's no activity that tugs on the heart-strings more than kicking a ball for your young so. So why do some parents do it? The answer is: in order to stay young.

"But that's daft!" say you. "Nobody can halt the march of time."

Well, you may not put it quite like that, but you'd be right. But then, you are an intelligent, rational-thinking child. Not an adult. As we've already established, adults don't think rationally, with or without an invisible hat. Therefore, what starts as a harmless game of football (is there any such thing as a harmless game of football these days?) turns into a battle for youthful supremacy. A battle that you, as the youth, are probably totally unaware is taking place. But it is.

Habitat:
The breed is to be found in the gym, at Weight Watchers, at cosmetic demonstrations in large department stores, and increasingly in the bathroom, in the sink, with an economy-sized bottle of Grecian 2000. Some dads who play a lot of football rub Cherry Blossom Shoe Polish on their hair. They're the ones who never head the ball!

Appearance:
This is the reverse of the Obvious Parent. Instead of you looking like them, the Youthful Parent struggles valiantly to look like you. They take an unusually keen interest in fashion. But this is not so they can advise you on your dress sense. It is so that they can tell you that your favourite dress, skirt, shirt, pair of trousers, etc, is out of fashion.

127

Shortly afterwards the particular item of clothing disappears. After an indecent pause, you find them wearing something very similar, but different somehow. In fact, it's dyed and doesn't fit. But don't let it depress you. The reason that it disappeared, and the reason that it has reappeared in disguise, is because you looked really *wicked* in it. Of course, by the time you read this book, *wicked* will probably be the outest word that it's possible to use. So I'll apologize in advance. (Of course, if you have found this book in one of those time capsule things, where it has been placed in order to give future generations, or alien life-forms, a clear indication of the sort of literature that we fell over ourselves to read in the twentieth century, then you will probably have given up reading long before you reached this page. Unless martians read backwards, like the Chinese. If you are an alien life-form you will probably already be familiar with Spock's Baby Book. So this may well be right up your street.)

Conversation:
Conversation with the Youthful Parent can be more scoffing than talking:

> "Huh! You're never going out looking like that," says Mum jealously.
> "Twenty press-ups? Make it two thousand and I'll accept the challenge," says Dad, pulling in his beer-gut.

Then, of course, there's the wistful:

> "I see flares are coming back in," says Dad, remembering that suitcaseful in the attic.
> "Purple hair would make a nice change." I think that was Mum!

Why this breed is dangerous:
I'm not sure whether they are more of a danger to you or themselves. They could do themselves permanent injury trying to keep up with you, but you would die of embarrassment being seen with them. And, as A Doctor wrote earlier, it is possible to die of embarrassment.

Z is for
Zealous Parent

The nature of the beast:
Zealous can mean keen and enthusiastic. It can also mean earnest. And it is this meaning that we are now concerned with: the Earnest or Zealous Parent. The Parent who is concerned with your inner well-being, whatever that means. Now, you know better than I do that being a teenager, or nearly a teenager, can be almost as confusing as this last sentence. The last thing you need is someone asking you how you *feel*. One of the problems with being young is that half the time you don't *know* how you feel. Actually, it's one of the problems with being *old*, as well (apparently!).

Habitat:
This particular breed of parent can be found almost anywhere that you have gone to be alone and quiet. You have sneaked away for a little ponder, and suddenly you are aware of an extra pair of eyes, staring at you, trying to read your mind. You see, a lot of these parents grew up in the Swinging Sixties, when everyone was trying to get into everyone else's head (and bed apparently, but that's another story). "I want to get into your *head*, man," was the common cry. I never worked out what it meant. I probably really missed out. Who knows?

But this explains why they still have the habit. They want to *understand* you. Why? They don't even understand themselves. And, anyway, do you want them to understand you? Of course you don't! You just want them to leave you alone!

Appearance:
Intense. And probably a bit "sixties".

Conversation:
This also tends to be intense. The Zealous Parent tries to draw your inner thoughts out of you, like someone trying to remove a reluctant winkle. In fact, *winkle* is a very good word for the Zealous Parent. They winkle a lot. Conversations go something like:

> **You**: I didn't do too well in the test today. (*Pause as the Zealous Parent stares at you*)
> **Parent**: Why do you think that was?
> **You**: I suppose because I didn't get some of the questions right.
> **Parent**: What do you think the *reason* was?
> **You**: Reason? Because I got them wrong, I suppose.
> **Parent**: Yes, but why do you think you got the questions wrong?
> **You**: Because I didn't know the right answers.
> **Parent**: Yes, but what do you think is the deep-seated underlying reason for your poor performance at this moment in time?
> **You**: Erm . . .

You think. You ponder. You dredge in the furthest, deepest corners of your mind. All the while the enquiring eyes of your Zealous Parent bore into your brain. At last, you think you may have discovered it. The underlying reason for your failure.

You: Er . . .
Parent: (*Eagerly*) Yes?
You: I think . . .
Parent: (*More eagerly*) Yes?
You: I think the reason might be . . .
Parent: (*Even more eagerly*) Yes?
You: I think it might be that I'm just not very good at sums.

Why this breed is dangerous:
Confusing is probably more the word, rather than dangerous.

Conclusion

In the previous pages I have outlined twenty-six of the existing parental types. There are more. Many, many more. There are as many as there as pebbles on a beach, stars in the sky, or, more properly, parents. For each parent is unique. Each parent is peculiar to themselves. Each parent is peculiar, anyway.

You may well have recognized your Mum and/or Dad from the previous descriptions. But, having identified them, having realized why they are like they are, what can be done about them?

Not very much, I'm afraid. You see, blood is thicker than water, and parents are even thicker. So trying to change them, adapt them, or even house-train them is an impossible task. But there are ways in which you can limit the effect they have on your life. For example:

Continual Questioning/Nagging
Should you be unfortunate enough to have a Nagging Parent, an Inquisitive Parent, or any of the other categories that involve excessive ear bashing, my advice is

to stay shtum. Say nothing. Flatly refuse to answer any question unless your lawyer is present. That usually puts them off.

Embarrassing Parents
If your particular parent is given to suddenly producing pictures of you as a baby, etc, the trick is to pretend that the photographs are not of you. One of the things that parents fear most is losing their memory, because it's a sure sign that they are getting old. You'll find that you don't have to work too hard to convince them that they are going senile. It is usually guaranteed to shut them up for weeks. Or at least until they have visited the doctor to be reassured (if they can remember where the doctor lives, of course!). The alternative is to get hold of a few photographs of *them*, and produce these at the right moment. A bit like playing snap.

> **Dad**: Now here's one of her on the beach, looking very silly.
> **You**: (*producing photo*) Snap!

Let's face it, you're far more likely to be able to get hold of a photo of your dad looking a wally than you are to get one of him looking sensible! You could also play a game of Embarrassing Photo Poker:

> **Dad**: Here's one of you with a bare bottom.
> **You**: OK. I'll see your bare bottom, and raise you a pair of flares.

It works every time!

Affectionate Obvious Parents
If your parents are given to unwanted bursts of affection in public, there is something you can try. At the first signs of a move in your direction, say, loud enough for other

people to hear: "You haven't ever had (*Name of Nasty Disease*) have you, Dad?" Any disease will do. Mumps works pretty well. Of course, if you're being descended on by a gaggle of old aunts at Christmas, you may have to resort to Bubonic Plague.

Actually this technique will also work in shops, if your Mum is trying to buy you unwanted new clothes:

> **Assistant**: Would you like to try it on, dear?
> **Dear**: (*That's you*) Yes, please. After all, the blouse won't get infected as long as I don't knock the scabs off any of my pustules.

This also works very well for making shop assistants sick. But that would be unfair. After all, they are only doing their job. They are very nice people, at home. It's just that they are *trained* to be condescending to anyone under twenty.

Of course the best thing you can do to counteract the affects of parental behaviour is to pretend to be busy, and therefore not really listening. Obviously this only works for a short time. Feeding the rabbit, bathing the dog or lancing the cat's boil can only be really spun out to last a few hours. (Although Randle Axminster of Welwyn Garden City once kept his parents out of his hair for four years by pretending to teach his grass snake to speak German, but I don't think this would work for everyone. Actually, Randle made the mistake of *actually* teaching his grass snake to speak German.)

You could try telling them that you're busy in the garden shed making a towel holder. In my experience that can take years. A sponsored silence is another really good idea. A sponsored breath-holding is a really bad idea. I suppose the short answer is to play each situation by ear. But remember, however devious you get, your parents may still outwit you, for theirs is not a logical thought process.

135

And Finally
However you decide to resolve the problem of coping with your parents, bear in mind that you will probably be a parent yourself one day. Then you can get your own back!

Would You Make a Good Parent?

Tackle this simple problem:

Your child is doing its homework. You can tell by the steam coming from its ears that it's having trouble. Do you:

A) Say: "Give it here. It can't be that difficult. We'll do it together"?

B) Say "Huh! When I was your age we had ten hours' worth of homework a night. And my Mum made me do it standing in a bowl of custard."

C) Hit them on the nose with a rolled-up newspaper.

Answers overleaf.

Answers:

If you answered A:
You do not really have what it takes to be a good parent. You see, it was a slightly trick question. Normally a parent would not realize that steam from their child's ears was a sign of it being in difficulty. They would naturally assume that it meant that their child was going down with some childhood complaint and do nothing about it. Also the average parent would know better than to help with homework, since they know that getting the answers wrong could lead to their child being kept in after school, and they wouldn't fancy doing that.

If you answered B:
This is a bit more like it. You obviously realize that it is very important for a good parent to instil in their child the difficulties that the parent had to struggle through to get to where they are today, even if where they are today is absolutely nowhere at all. The custard may be stretching credibility slightly, though. Particularly if it's anything like my mother's custard. Nothing could stand up in that and live to tell the tale.

If you answered C:
Well done! You clearly see the need for discipline. This, coupled with a balanced diet and regular walks, will ensure that your child has a wet nose and a glossy coat. These are basic requirement, particularly if you are thinking of showing them or putting them to stud, some time in the future.

138

Other books by the same author

THE COMPLETE WORKS OF SHAKESPEARE*

SCOUTING FOR BOYS*

THE BIBLE*

A HUNDRED AND ONE USES FOR A SINGLE PIECE OF OLD CHEWING GUM*

A SINGLE USE FOR A HUNDRED AND ONE PIECES OF OLD CHEWING GUM*

CREATIVE KNITTING WITH SPAGHETTI*

CERAMIC VASES*

★ ★ ★ ★ ★

WHAT SOME REALLY FAMOUS PEOPLE HAVE SAID ABOUT THIS BOOK:

"This book was much taller when it was a tree." T S ELIOT*

"There's only one word for this book: totally fantastic!" SIR RICHARD ATTENBOROUGH*

"I wish I could write books like this." JEFFREY ARCHER*

"I haven't read it." PETER COREY*

"The spelling is terrific!" RONALD DALL*

* NOT REALLY!